Supplemental Liturgical Texts

Prayer Book Studies 30

The Standing Liturgical Commission
of the Episcopal Church

The Church Hymnal Corporation
800 Second Avenue, New York, NY 10017

Acknowledgments

The translations of the Gloria Patri, Benedictus Dominus Deus, Magnificat, Te Deum laudamus, Gloria in excelsis, Apostles' Creed, Lord's Prayer, Suffrages C at Morning Prayer, Nicene Creed, and Sursum corda used in this book are those proposed to the churches by the ecumenical English Language Liturgical Consultation (ELLC). Copyright © 1987, ELLC. All rights reserved.

Grateful acknowledgement is made for permission to use the following settings of the Sanctus: Hurd, *New Plainsong,* copyright © 1982, G.I.A. Publications, Inc.; Proulx, *A Community Mass,* copyright © 1971, 1977, G.I.A. Publications, Inc.; Mathias, copyright © 1976, Oxford University Press, Inc.; Schubert/Proulx, *Deutsche Messe* adaptation, copyright © 1985, G.I.A. Publications, Inc. The Musical Supplement was prepared by the Standing Commission on Church Music.

Published for the Standing Liturgical Commission of The Episcopal Church by the Church Hymnal Corporation, 800 Second Avenue, New York, New York 10017.

Table of Contents

The directions "Concerning the Service" and "Concerning the Celebration" on pages 74, 108, and 354 of The Book of Common Prayer apply also to the services in this book.

Preface

The language of Christian liturgical prayer springs from the deep wells of Scripture, tradition, and human experience—constantly changing and complex. The liturgies of the Church have always drawn from many sources to communicate and celebrate the truth of our lives in Jesus Christ in the clearest, most compelling way possible. The effectiveness and endurability of prayer is contingent upon how well its images, words, and metaphors convey both the depth and mystery of the Gospel, and the voice and heart of the worshiping community. The common prayer of the Church emerges from the faith community and in turn, the community is formed and shaped by that prayer.

The services in *Prayer Book Studies 30—Supplemental Liturgical Texts* also have as their source these distinct but entirely linked currents of prayer. While the Offices and Holy Eucharist will be readily recognized as familiar forms of Anglican prayer, structured in familiar sequence, they also reflect the increasing sensitivity of the English language itself that certain words, images, and phrases are changing in meaning, particularly those which contain reference to gender. And, importantly, they also reflect substantive biblical study that has begun to awaken the Church to a wealth of images and metaphors for God which have not previously been articulated in the liturgy.

These texts, then, contain much that is familiar; some revisions which render biblical passages closer to the wording of the original language; and additional biblical images and passages which provide an expanded sense of the person of God and the worshiping community. In so doing, they engage the Church in the privilege and responsibility which every generation has to search for and speak of the evolving human experience in its relationship to the permanent truths of God. Such searching, which is the heart of the spiritual life, cannot help but be reflected in the language with which the prayer is offered.

Nowhere is the sensitivity to the basic truth that every human being is created in the image of God as important as in the liturgy of the Church. The Gospel's call—and the Church's commitment—is to speak the word of grace and, in turn, to give voice to those who receive it. These services are part of the Church's age-old effort to raise up ever-new forms of prayer and praise from every corner of life. They seek to offer new ways of speaking the old truths: an invitation to venture into the deepening prayer life of the Church and into the renewing streams of salvation.

NOTE

All worshipers, and especially every liturgical leader, are invited and urged to participate in the continuing refinement of these services. They are provided as part of an on-going dialogue in the Church, under the direction of the Standing Liturgical Commission, about language and liturgy. In their present form, they are to be used under the authority of the diocesan bishop, whose office has further information regarding the evaluation process.
A full commentary on the texts has been published separately, with chapters containing material on the liturgical and theological background for the texts, rationales and biblical references, suggested guidelines, and a brief educational program. Use of this Commentary is strongly urged for greater understanding of these services. It may be purchased by contacting the Church Hymnal Corporation (800 Second Avenue, New York, New York 10017, 1-800-223-6602) or through Church bookstores.

The Daily Office

Concerning these Services

The forms of Daily Morning and Evening Prayer and Order of Worship for the Evening which follow are intended to manifest the emerging consensus that liturgical language should be as widely inclusive and representative of the variety of the human community as possible. They are not newly composed but are adaptations of the forms in the Book of Common Prayer. In many cases both the familiar Prayer Book forms and suggested alternatives are printed in the text, so that either may be used.

The majority of texts traditionally associated with Morning and Evening Prayer find their source in the Bible. The Psalms and most of the Canticles originate there; the appointed readings are also drawn from Scripture. Even the prayers of the Offices echo biblical texts. Often the language of the biblical translations used in the liturgy is not accurately translated, and therefore less inclusive than the wording of the original text. The work of adaptation has involved finding better translations of existing texts, and including new biblical texts.

For this adaptation it was determined that language referring to the human community should express inclusivity in all instances. For example, masculine pronouns are no longer used in phrases of general human reference.

Regarding language used in reference to God, the primary concern has been that of fidelity to biblical language. The biblical metaphors of *Father* and *Lord* have a fundamental place in Christian prayer and theology and have been retained, although their use is less frequent than in existing Prayer Book services. Other Scriptural images of God, including feminine images from the Wisdom literature, have been introduced.

"Honor and glory" is an alternative doxology expressing the praise of the Triune God which may be used in place of the Gloria Patri.

Canticle numbers ending with *A* identify adaptations of the Canticles with the corresponding number in the Book of Common Prayer. Canticles 21 and 22 are additions taken from the Wisdom literature.

Additional directions are on page 56.

Please see also Commentary on Prayer Book Studies 30, a companion volume, for background and reference material about these services.

Daily Morning Prayer:
Rite Two *Adapted*

The Officiant begins the service with one or more of these sentences of Scripture, or with one of the versicles on pages 12–13.

(The sentences and invitatory antiphons marked with an asterisk [*] are especially recommended for use with these services.)

Advent

Watch, for you do not know when the master of the house will come, in the evening, or at midnight, or at cockcrow, or in the morning, lest he come suddenly and find you asleep. *Mark 13:35, 36*

In the wilderness prepare the way of the LORD, make straight in the desert a highway for our God.   *Isaiah 40:3*

The glory of the LORD shall be revealed, and all flesh shall see it together.   *Isaiah 40:5*

* Arise, O Jerusalem, stand upon the height and look toward the east, and see your children gathered from west and east at the word of the Holy One.   *Baruch 5:5*

Christmas

Behold, I bring you good news of a great joy which will come to all the people; for to you is born this day in the city of David, a Savior, who is Christ the Lord.   *Luke 2:10, 11*

Behold, the dwelling of God is with humankind. He will dwell with them, and they shall be his people, and God himself will be with them, and be their God. *Revelation 21:3*

* The Word became flesh and dwelt among us, full of grace and truth. *John 1:14*

Epiphany

Nations shall come to your light, and kings to the brightness of your rising. *Isaiah 60:3*

* I will give you as a light to the nations, that my salvation may reach to the end of the earth. *Isaiah 49:6b*

From the rising of the sun to its setting my Name shall be great among the nations, and in every place incense shall be offered to my Name, and a pure offering; for my Name shall be great among the nations, says the LORD of hosts. *Malachi 1:11*

Lent

* If we say we have no sin, we deceive ourselves, and the truth is not in us, but if we confess our sins, God, who is faithful and just, will forgive our sins and cleanse us from all unrighteousness. *1 John 1:8, 9*

Rend your hearts and not your garments. Return to the LORD your God, for he is gracious and merciful, slow to anger and abounding in steadfast love, and repents of evil. *Joel 2:13*

I will arise and go to my father, and I will say to him, "Father, I have sinned against heaven and before you; I am no longer worthy to be called your son." *Luke 15:18, 19*

To the Lord our God belong mercy and forgiveness, because we have rebelled against him and have not obeyed the voice of the LORD our God by following his laws which he set before us. *Daniel 9:9, 10*

* Jesus said: "If any of you would come after me, deny yourself and take up your cross and follow me." *Mark 8:34*

Holy Week

All we like sheep have gone astray; we have turned every one to his own way; and the LORD has laid on him the iniquity of us all. *Isaiah 53:6*

Is it nothing to you, all you who pass by? Look and see if there is any sorrow like my sorrow which was brought upon me, whom the LORD has afflicted. *Lamentations 1:12*

* Christ Jesus, being found in human form, humbled himself and became obedient unto death, even death on a cross.
Philippians 2:8

Easter Season, including Ascension Day and the Day of Pentecost

Alleluia! Christ is risen.
The Lord is risen indeed. Alleluia!

On this day the LORD has acted; we will rejoice and be glad in it. *Psalm 118:24*

Thanks be to God, who gives us the victory through our Lord Jesus Christ. *1 Corinthians 15:57*

* If then you have been raised with Christ, seek the things that are above, where Christ is, seated at the right hand of God.
Colossians 3:1

* Christ has entered, not into a sanctuary made with hands, a copy of the true one, but into heaven itself, now to appear in the presence of God on our behalf.   *Hebrews 9:24*

* You shall receive power when the Holy Spirit has come upon you; and you shall be my witnesses in Jerusalem, and in all Judea, and Samaria, and to the ends of the earth.   *Acts 1:8*

Trinity Sunday

* Holy, holy, holy is the Lord God Almighty, who was, and is, and is to come!   *Revelation 4:8*

All Saints and other Major Saints' Days

We give thanks to the Father, who has made us worthy to share in the inheritance of the saints in light.   *Colossians 1:12*

* You are no longer strangers and sojourners, but citizens together with the saints and members of the household of God.   *Ephesians 2:19*

* Their sound has gone out into all lands, and their message to the ends of the world.   *Psalm 19:4*

Occasions of Thanksgiving

Give thanks to the LORD, and call upon his Name; make known his deeds among the peoples.   *Psalm 105:1*

* We give you thanks, O God, we give you thanks, calling upon your Name and declaring all your wonderful deeds. *Psalm 75:1*

At any Time

Grace to you and peace from God our Father and the Lord Jesus Christ.   *Philippians 1:2*

I was glad when they said to me, "Let us go to the house of the LORD." *Psalm 122:1*

Let the words of my mouth and the meditation of my heart be acceptable in your sight, O LORD, my strength and my redeemer. *Psalm 19:14*

* Send out your light and your truth, that they may lead me, and bring me to your holy hill and to your dwelling. *Psalm 43:3*

The LORD is in his holy temple; let all the earth keep silence before him. *Habakkuk 2:20*

The hour is coming, and now is, when the true worshipers will worship the Father in spirit and truth, for such the Father seeks to worship him. *John 4:23*

* Thus says the high and lofty One who inhabits eternity, whose name is Holy, "I dwell in the high and holy place and also with the one who has a contrite and humble spirit, to revive the spirit of the humble and to revive the heart of the contrite." *Isaiah 57:15*

* God is Spirit, and those who worship must worship in spirit and in truth. *John 4:24*

The following Confession of Sin may then be said; or the Office may continue at once with one of the versicles on pages 12–13.

Beloved in Christ, we have come together to proclaim God's praise, to hear God's holy Word, and to ask, for ourselves and on behalf of others, those things that are necessary for our life and our salvation. And so that we may prepare ourselves in heart and mind to worship God, let us kneel in silence, and with penitent and obedient hearts confess our sins, that by divine goodness and mercy we may obtain forgiveness.

or the following

Let us confess our sins against God and our neighbor.

Silence may be kept.

Officiant and People together, all kneeling

Most merciful God,
we confess that we have sinned against you
in thought, word, and deed,
by what we have done,
and by what we have left undone.
We have not loved you with our whole heart;
we have not loved our neighbors as ourselves.
We are truly sorry and we humbly repent.
For the sake of our Savior Jesus Christ,
have mercy on us and forgive us;
that we may delight in your will,
and walk in your ways,
to the glory of your Name. Amen.

The Priest alone stands and says

Almighty God have mercy on you, forgive you all your sins
through the grace of Jesus Christ, strengthen you in all
goodness, and by the power of the Holy Spirit keep you in
eternal life. *Amen.*

*A deacon or lay person using the preceding form remains kneeling, and
substitutes "us" for "you" and "our" for "your."*

The Invitatory and Psalter

All stand

Officiant	O God, let our mouth proclaim your praise.
People	And your glory all the day long.

or the following

Officiant Lord, open our lips.
People And our mouth shall proclaim your praise.

Officiant and People

Glory to the Father, and to the Son, and to the Holy Spirit; as it was in the beginning, is now, and will be for ever. Amen.

Except in Lent, add Alleluia.

or this

Honor and glory to the holy and undivided Trinity, God who creates, redeems, and inspires: One in Three and Three in One, for ever and ever. Amen.

Except in Lent, add Alleluia.

Then follows one of the Invitatory Psalms, Venite or Jubilate.

One of the following Antiphons may be sung or said with the Venite or Jubilate.

In Advent

* Our God and Savior now draws near: O come let us worship.

On the twelve days of Christmas

* Alleluia. To us a child is born: O come let us worship.

From the Epiphany through the Baptism of Christ, and on the Feasts of the Transfiguration and Holy Cross

* Christ has shown forth his glory: O come let us worship.

In Lent

* Our God is full of compassion and mercy: O come let us worship.

or the following

* Today, if you would hear God's voice: harden not your hearts.

From Easter Day until the Ascension

Alleluia. The Lord is risen indeed: O come let us worship. Alleluia.

or this

* Alleluia. Christ is risen: O come let us worship. Alleluia.

From Ascension Day until the Day of Pentecost

* Alleluia. Christ the Lord has ascended into heaven: O come let us worship. Alleluia.

On the Day of Pentecost

* Alleluia. The Spirit of God renews the face of the earth: O come let us worship. Alleluia.

On Trinity Sunday

* The holy and undivided Trinity, one God: O come let us worship.

On other Sundays

* Christ has triumphed over death: O come let us worship.

On other Sundays and weekdays

The earth is the Lord's, for he made it: O come let us worship.

or this

Worship the Lord in the beauty of holiness: O come let us worship.

or this

The mercy of the Lord is everlasting: O come let us worship.

or the following

* God is the Rock of our salvation: O come let us worship.

  or this

* The Holy One is in our midst: O come let us worship.

  The alleluias in the following Antiphons are used only in Easter Season.

  On Feasts of the Incarnation

* [Alleluia.] The Word was made flesh and dwelt among us: O come let us worship. [Alleluia.]

  On All Saints and other Major Saints' Days

* [Alleluia.] Our God is glorious in all the saints: O come let us worship. [Alleluia.]

Venite   *Psalm 95:1–7*

Come, let us sing to the LORD, *
   let us shout for joy to the Rock of our salvation.
Let us come before his presence with thanksgiving *
   and raise a loud shout to him with psalms.

For the LORD is a great God, *
   and a great King above all gods.
In his hand are the caverns of the earth, *
   and the heights of the hills are his also.
The sea is his, for he made it, *
   and his hands have molded the dry land.

Come, let us bow down, and bend the knee, *
   and kneel before the LORD our Maker.
For he is our God,
and we are the people of his pasture and the sheep
                  of his hand. *
   Oh, that today you would hearken to God's voice!

or Psalm 95, Prayer Book, page 724

Jubilate *Psalm 100*

[Book of Common Prayer, page 82]

*In place of an Invitatory Psalm, the following Morning Psalm may be
sung or said.*

Psalm 63 *Deus, Deus meus*

O God, you are my God; eagerly I seek you; *
    my soul thirsts for you, my flesh faints for you,
    as in a barren and dry land where there is no water.
Therefore I have gazed upon you in your holy place, *
    that I might behold your power and your glory.
For your loving-kindness is better than life itself; *
    my lips shall give you praise.
So will I bless you as long as I live *
    and lift up my hands in your Name.
My soul is content, as with marrow and fatness, *
    and my mouth praises you with joyful lips,
When I remember you upon my bed, *
    and meditate on you in the night watches.
For you have been my helper, *
    and under the shadow of your wings I will rejoice.
My soul clings to you; *
    your right hand holds me fast.

*In Easter Week, in place of an Invitatory Psalm, or Psalm 63, the
following is sung or said. It may also be used daily until the Day of
Pentecost.*

Christ our Passover *Pascha nostrum*

1 Corinthians 5:7–8; Romans 6:9–11; 1 Corinthians 15:20–22

[Book of Common Prayer, page 83]

Then follows

The Psalm or Psalms Appointed

At the end of the Psalms is sung or said

Glory to the Father, and to the Son, and to the Holy
Spirit; as it was in the beginning, is now, and will be for
ever. Amen.

or this

Honor and glory to the holy and undivided Trinity, *
    God who creates, redeems, and inspires:
One in Three and Three in One, *
    for ever and ever. Amen.

The Lessons

One or two Lessons, as appointed, are read, the Reader first saying

A Reading (Lesson) from _____ .

A citation giving chapter and verse may be added.

After each Lesson the Reader may say

            The Word of the Lord.
Answer   Thanks be to God.

Or the Reader may say   Here ends the Lesson (Reading).

*Silence may be kept after each Reading. One of the following Canticles or
one of the Canticles found on pages 85–96 of the Book of Common
Prayer is sung or said after each Reading. If three Lessons are used, the
Lesson from the Gospel is read after the second Canticle.*

9A The First Song of Isaiah *Ecce, Deus*

Isaiah 12:2–6

Surely, it is God who saves me; *
   I will trust and will not be afraid.
For the LORD is my stronghold and my sure defense, *
   and he will be my Savior.
Therefore you shall draw water with rejoicing *
   from the springs of salvation.
And on that day you shall say, *
   Give thanks to the LORD and call upon his Name;
Make his deeds known among the peoples; *
   see that they remember that his Name is exalted.
Sing the praises of the LORD, for he has done great things, *
   and this is known in all the world.
Cry aloud, inhabitants of Zion, ring out your joy, *
   for the great one in the midst of you is the Holy One
              of Israel.

12A A Song of Creation *Benedicite, omnia opera Domini*

Song of the Three Young Men, 35–65

One or more sections of this Canticle may be used. Whatever the
selection, it begins with the Invocation and concludes with the Doxology.

Invocation

Glorify the Lord, all you works of the Lord, *
    sing praise and give honor for ever.
In the high vault of heaven, glorify the Lord, *
    sing praise and give honor for ever.

I The Cosmic Order

Glorify the Lord, you angels and all powers of the Lord, *
    O heavens and all waters above the heavens.
Sun and moon and stars of the sky, glorify the Lord, *
    sing praise and give honor for ever.

Glorify the Lord, every shower of rain and fall of dew, *
    all winds and fire and heat.
Winter and summer, glorify the Lord, *
    sing praise and give honor for ever.

Glorify the Lord, O chill and cold, *
    drops of dew and flakes of snow.
Frost and cold, ice and sleet, glorify the Lord, *
    sing praise and give honor for ever.

Glorify the Lord, O nights and days, *
    O shining light and enfolding dark.
Storm clouds and thunderbolts, glorify the Lord, *
    sing praise and give honor for ever.

II The Earth and its Creatures

Let the earth glorify the Lord, *
    sing praise and give honor for ever.

Glorify the Lord, O mountains and hills,
and all that grows upon the earth, *
   sing praise and give honor for ever.

Glorify the Lord, O springs of water, seas, and streams, *
   O whales and all that move in the waters.
All birds of the air, glorify the Lord, *
   sing praise and give honor for ever.

Glorify the Lord, O beasts of the wild, *
   and all you flocks and herds.
O men and women everywhere, glorify the Lord, *
   sing praise and give honor for ever.

III   *The People of God*

Let the people of God glorify the Lord, *
   sing praise and give honor for ever.
Glorify the Lord, O priests and servants of the Lord, *
   sing praise and give honor for ever.

Glorify the Lord, O spirits and souls of the righteous, *
   sing praise and give honor for ever.
You that are holy and humble of heart, glorify the Lord, *
   sing praise and give honor for ever.

Doxology

Let us glorify the Lord: Father, Son, and Holy Spirit; *
   sing praise and give honor for ever.
In the high vault of heaven, glorify the Lord, *
   sing praise and give honor for ever.

13A   A Song of Praise   *Benedictus es, Domine*
Song of the Three Young Men, 29–34

Glory to you, Lord God of our forebears; *
     you are worthy of praise; glory to you.
Glory to you for the radiance of your holy Name; *
     we will praise you and highly exalt you for ever.

Glory to you in the splendor of your temple; *
     on the throne of your majesty, glory to you.
Glory to you, seated between the Cherubim; *
     we will praise you and highly exalt you for ever.

Glory to you, beholding the depths; *
     in the high vault of heaven, glory to you.
Glory to you, Father, Son, and Holy Spirit; *
     we will praise you and highly exalt you for ever.

14A   A Song of Penitence   *Kyrie Pantokrator*
Prayer of Manasseh, 1–2, 4, 6–7, 11–15

Especially suitable in Lent, and on other penitential occasions

O Lord and Ruler of the hosts of heaven, *
     God of Abraham, Isaac, and Jacob,
     and of all their righteous offspring:
You made the heavens and the earth, *
     with all their vast array.
All things quake with fear at your presence; *
     they tremble because of your power.
But your merciful promise is beyond all measure; *
     it surpasses all that our minds can fathom.
O Most High, you are full of compassion, *
     long-suffering and abounding in mercy.

You hold back your hand; *
   you do not punish as we deserve.
In your great goodness, Lord,
you have promised forgiveness to sinners, *
   that they may repent of their sin and be saved.
And now, I bend the knee of my heart, *
   and make my appeal, sure of your gracious goodness.
I have sinned, O Lord, I have sinned, *
   and I know my wickedness only too well.
Therefore I make this prayer to you: *
   Forgive me, Lord, forgive me.
Do not let me perish in my sin, *
   nor condemn me to the depths of the earth.
For you, O Lord, are the God of those who repent, *
   and in me you will show forth your goodness.
Unworthy as I am, you will save me,
in accordance with your great mercy, *
   and I will praise you without ceasing all the days
            of my life.
For all the powers of heaven sing your praises, *
   and yours is the glory to ages of ages. Amen.

15A   The Song of Mary   *Magnificat*

Luke 1:46–55

My soul proclaims the greatness of the Lord,
my spirit rejoices in God my Savior, *
   for you, Lord, have looked with favor on your lowly servant.
From this day all generations will call me blessed: *
   you, the Almighty, have done great things for me,
   and holy is your name.

You have mercy on those who fear you *
   from generation to generation.
You have shown strength with your arm *
   and scattered the proud in their conceit,
Casting down the mighty from their thrones *
   and lifting up the lowly.
You have filled the hungry with good things *
   and sent the rich away empty.
You have come to the aid of your servant Israel, *
   to remember the promise of mercy,
The promise made to our forebears, *
   to Abraham and his children for ever.

16A   The Song of Zechariah   *Benedictus Dominus Deus*

Luke 1:68–79

Blessed are you, Lord, the God of Israel, *
   you have come to your people and set them free.
You have raised up for us a mighty Savior, *
   born of the house of your servant David.
Through your holy prophets you promised of old
to save us from our enemies, *
   from the hands of all who hate us.
To show mercy to our forebears, *
   and to remember your holy covenant.
This was the oath you swore to our father Abraham: *
   to set us free from the hands of our enemies,
Free to worship you without fear, *
   holy and righteous before you,
   all the days of our life.

And you, child, shall be called the prophet of the
        Most High, *
  for you will go before the Lord to prepare the way,
To give God's people knowledge of salvation *
  by the forgiveness of their sins.
In the tender compassion of our God *
  the dawn from on high shall break upon us,
To shine on those who dwell in darkness and the shadow
        of death, *
  and to guide our feet into the way of peace.

18A   A Song to the Lamb   *Dignus es*

Revelation 4:11; 5:9–10, 13

Splendor and honor and royal power *
  are yours by right, O God Most High,
For you created everything that is, *
  and by your will they were created and have their being;

And yours by right, O Lamb that was slain, *
  for with your blood you have redeemed for God,
From every family, language, people, and nation, *
  a royal priesthood to serve our God.

And so, to the One who sits upon the throne, *
  and to Christ the Lamb,
Be worship and praise, dominion and splendor, *
  for ever and for evermore.

20A Glory to God *Gloria in excelsis*

Glory to God in the highest,
and peace to God's people on earth.

Lord God, heavenly King,
almighty God and Father,
we worship you, we give you thanks,
we praise you for your glory.

Lord Jesus Christ, only Son of the Father,
Lord God, Lamb of God,
you take away the sin of the world:
have mercy on us;
you are seated at the right hand of the Father:
receive our prayer.

For you alone are the Holy One,
you alone are the Lord,
you alone are the Most High,
Jesus Christ,
with the Holy Spirit,
in the glory of God the Father. Amen.

21A You are God *Te Deum laudamus*

We praise you, O God,
we acclaim you as Lord;
all creation worships you,
the Father everlasting.
To you all angels, all the powers of heaven,
the cherubim and seraphim, sing in endless praise:
    Holy, holy, holy Lord, God of power and might,
    heaven and earth are full of your glory.
The glorious company of apostles praise you.
The noble fellowship of prophets praise you.
The white-robed army of martyrs praise you.
Throughout the world the holy Church acclaims you:
    Father, of majesty unbounded,
    your true and only Son, worthy of all praise,
    the Holy Spirit, advocate and guide.

You, Christ, are the king of glory,
the eternal Son of the Father.
When you took our flesh to set us free
you humbly chose the Virgin's womb.
You overcame the sting of death
and opened the kingdom of heaven to all believers.
You are seated at God's right hand in glory.
We believe that you will come to be our judge.
    Come then, Lord, and help your people,
    bought with the price of your own blood,
    and bring us with your saints
    to glory everlasting.

22 A Song of Wisdom *Sapientia liberavit*

Wisdom 10:15–19, 20b–21

Wisdom freed from a nation of oppressors *
  a holy people and a blameless race.
She entered the soul of a servant of the Lord, *
  withstood dread rulers with wonders and signs.

To the saints she gave the reward of their labors, *
  and led them by a marvelous way;
She was their shelter by day *
  and a blaze of stars by night.

She brought them across the Red Sea, *
  she led them through mighty waters;
But their enemies she swallowed in the waves *
  and spewed them out from the depths of the abyss.

And then, Lord, the righteous sang hymns to your Name, *
  and praised with one voice your protecting hand;
For Wisdom opened the mouths of the mute, *
  and gave speech to the tongues of a new-born people.

23 A Song of Pilgrimage *Priusquam errarem*

Ecclesiasticus 51:13–22

Before I ventured forth,
even while I was very young, *
  I sought wisdom openly in my prayer.

In the forecourts of the temple I asked for her, *
    and I will seek her to the end.
From first blossom to early fruit, *
    she has been the delight of my heart.
My foot has kept firmly to the true path, *
    diligently from my youth have I pursued her.
I inclined my ear a little and received her; *
    I found for myself much wisdom and became adept in her.
To the one who gives me wisdom will I give glory, *
    for I have resolved to live according to her way.
I have been zealous for the good, *
    in order that I might not be put to shame.
My soul has been subdued by her, *
    and I have been careful in my conduct.
I spread out my hands to the heavens, *
    and lamented my ignorance of her.
I directed my soul to her, *
    and through purification have I found her.
From the beginning I gained courage from her, *
    therefore I will not be forsaken.
In my inmost being have I been stirred to seek her, *
    therefore have I gained a good possession.
As my reward the Almighty has given me the gift
                of language, *
    and with it will I offer praise to God.

The Apostles' Creed

Officiant and People together, all standing

I believe in God, the Father almighty,
   creator of heaven and earth.
I believe in Jesus Christ, God's only Son, our Lord,
   who was conceived by the Holy Spirit,
   born of the Virgin Mary,
   suffered under Pontius Pilate,
   was crucified, died, and was buried;
   he descended to the dead.
   On the third day he rose again;
   he ascended into heaven,
   he is seated at the right hand of the Father,
   and he will come again to judge the living and the dead.
I believe in the Holy Spirit,
   the holy catholic Church,
   the communion of saints,
   the forgiveness of sins,
   the resurrection of the body,
   and the life everlasting. Amen.

The Prayers

The people stand or kneel

Officiant   Hear our cry, O God.
People   And listen to our prayer.
Officiant   Let us pray.

or this

Officiant   The Lord be with you.
People   And also with you.
Officiant   Let us pray.

Our Father in heaven,
   hallowed be your Name,
   your kingdom come,
   your will be done,
      on earth as in heaven.
Give us today our daily bread.
Forgive us our sins
   as we forgive those who sin against us.
Save us from the time of trial,
   and deliver us from evil.
For the kingdom, the power, and the glory are yours,
   now and for ever. Amen.

Then follows one of these sets of Suffrages

A

V.   Show us your mercy, O Lord;
R.   And grant us your salvation.
V.   Clothe your ministers with righteousness;
R.   Let your people sing with joy.
V.   Give peace, O Lord, in all the world;
R.   For only in you can we live in safety.
V.   Lord, keep this nation under your care;
R.   And guide us in the way of justice and truth.
V.   Let your way be known upon earth;
R.   Your saving health among all nations.
V.   Let not the needy, O Lord, be forgotten;
R.   Nor the hope of the poor be taken away.
V.   Create in us clean hearts, O God;
R.   And sustain us with your Holy Spirit.

B

V. Help us, O God our Savior;
R. Deliver us and forgive us our sins.
V. Look upon your congregation;
R. Give to your people the blessing of peace.
V. Declare your glory among the nations;
R. And your wonders among all peoples.
V. Let not the oppressed be shamed and turned away;
R. Never forget the lives of your poor.
V. Continue your loving-kindness to those who know you;
R. And your favor to those who are true of heart.
V. Satisfy us by your loving-kindness in the morning;
R. So shall we rejoice and be glad all the days of our life.

C

V. Save your people, Lord, and bless your inheritance;
R. Govern and uphold them now and always.
V. Day by day we bless you;
R. We praise your Name for ever.
V. Keep us today, Lord, from all sin.
R. Have mercy on us, Lord, have mercy.
V. Lord, show us your love and mercy;
R. For we have put our trust in you,
V. In you, Lord, is our hope;
R. Let us never be put to shame.

The Officiant then says one or more of the following Collects

The Collect of the Day

A Collect for Sundays

O God, you make us glad with the weekly remembrance of the glorious resurrection of your Son: Give us this day such blessing through our worship of you, that the week to come may be spent in your favor; through Jesus Christ our Lord. *Amen.*

A Collect for Fridays

Almighty God, whose most dear Son went not up to joy but first he suffered pain, and entered not into glory before he was crucified: Mercifully grant that we, walking in the way of the cross, may find it none other than the way of life and peace; through Jesus Christ our Savior. *Amen.*

A Collect for Saturdays

Almighty God, who after the creation of the world rested from all your works and sanctified a day of rest for all your creatures: Grant that we, putting away all earthly anxieties, may be duly prepared for the service of your sanctuary, and that our rest here upon earth may be a preparation for the eternal rest promised to your people in heaven; through Jesus Christ our Savior. *Amen.*

A Collect for the Renewal of Life

Eternal God, whose light divides the day from the night and turns the shadow of death into the morning: Drive far from us all wrong desires, incline our hearts to keep your law, and guide our feet into the way of peace; that, having done your will with cheerfulness during the day, we may, when night comes, rejoice to give you thanks; through Jesus Christ our Savior. *Amen.*

A Collect for Peace

O God, the author of peace and lover of concord, to know you is eternal life and to serve you is perfect freedom: Defend us, your humble servants, in all assaults of our enemies; that we, surely trusting in your defense, may not fear the power of any adversaries; through the might of Jesus Christ our Lord. *Amen.*

A Collect for Grace

Almighty and everlasting God, you have brought us in safety to this new day: preserve us with your mighty power, that we may not fall into sin, nor be overcome by adversity; and in all we do, direct us to the fulfilling of your purpose; through Jesus Christ our Savior. *Amen.*

A Collect for Guidance

O God, our Creator and Sustainer, in you we live and move and have our being: We humbly pray you so to guide and govern us by your Holy Spirit, that in all the cares and occupations of our life we may not forget you, but may remember that we are ever walking in your sight; through Jesus Christ our Lord. *Amen.*

Then, unless the Eucharist or a form of general intercession is to follow, one of the following prayers for mission is added

Almighty and everlasting God, by whose Spirit the whole body of your faithful people is governed and sanctified: Receive our supplications and prayers which we offer before you for all members of your holy Church, that in their vocation and ministry they may truly and devoutly serve you; through our Lord and Savior Jesus Christ. *Amen.*

or the following

O God, you have made of one blood all the peoples of the earth, and sent your blessed Son to preach peace to those who are far off and to those who are near: Grant that people everywhere may seek after you and find you; bring the nations into your fold; pour out your Spirit upon all flesh; and hasten the coming of your kingdom; through Jesus Christ our Lord. *Amen.*

or this

Lord Jesus Christ, you stretched out your arms of love on the hard wood of the cross that everyone might come within the reach of your saving embrace: So clothe us in your Spirit that we, reaching forth our hands in love, may bring those who do not know you to the knowledge and love of you; for the honor of your Name. *Amen.*

Here may be sung a hymn or anthem.

Authorized intercessions and thanksgivings may follow.

Before the close of the Office one or both of the following may be used

The General Thanksgiving

Officiant and People

Almighty God, Father of all mercies,
we your unworthy servants give you humble thanks
for all your goodness and loving-kindness
to us and to all whom you have made.
We bless you for our creation, preservation,
and all the blessings of this life;
but above all for your immeasurable love
in the redemption of the world by our Lord Jesus Christ;
for the means of grace, and for the hope of glory.
And, we pray, give us such an awareness of your mercies,
that with truly thankful hearts we may show forth your praise,

not only with our lips, but in our lives,
by giving up our selves to your service,
and by walking before you
in holiness and righteousness all our days;
through Jesus Christ our Lord,
to whom, with you and the Holy Spirit,
be honor and glory throughout all ages. Amen.

A Prayer of St. Chrysostom

Jesus our Savior, you have given us grace at this time with
one accord to make our common supplication to you; and
you have promised that when two or three are agreed in your
Name you will grant their requests: Fulfill now, O Lord, our
desires and petitions as may be best for us; granting us in this
world knowledge of your truth, and in the age to come life
everlasting. *Amen.*

Then may be said

Let us bless the Lord.
Thanks be to God.

*From Easter Day through the Day of Pentecost "Alleluia, alleluia" may be
added to the preceding versicle and response.*

The Officiant may then conclude with one of the following

The grace of our Lord Jesus Christ, and the love of God, and
the fellowship of the Holy Spirit, be with us all evermore.
Amen.   *2 Corinthians 13:14*

May the God of hope fill us with all joy and peace in
believing through the power of the Holy Spirit. *Amen.*
Romans 15:13

Glory to God whose power, working in us, can do infinitely
more than we can ask or imagine: Glory to God from
generation to generation in the Church, and in Christ Jesus
for ever and ever. *Amen.*   *Ephesians 3:20, 21*

An Order of Worship
for the Evening *Adapted*

The church is dark, or partially so, when the service is to begin.

All stand, and the Officiant greets the people with these words

> Light and peace, in Jesus Christ our Lord.
People > Thanks be to God.

In place of the above, from Easter Day through the Day of Pentecost

Officiant Christ has risen as he promised. Alleluia!
People And has appeared to the disciples. Alleluia!

or this

Officiant Stay with us, Christ, for it is evening. Alleluia!
People Illumine your Church with your radiance. Alleluia!

In Lent and on other penitential occasions

Officiant Blessed be the God of our salvation.
People Who bears our burdens and forgives our sins.

One of the following, or some other Short Lesson of Scripture appropriate to the occasion or to the season, may then be read

Jesus said, "You are the light of the world. A city built on a hill cannot be hid. No one lights a lamp to put it under a bucket, but on a lamp-stand where it gives light for everyone in the house. And you, like the lamp, must shed light among other people, so that they may see the good you do, and give glory to your Father in heaven." *Matthew 5:14–16*

What we preach is not ourselves, but Jesus Christ as Lord, with ourselves as your servants for Jesus' sake. For it is the God who said, "Let light shine out of darkness," who has shone in our hearts to give the light of knowledge of the glory of God in the face of Christ.   *2 Corinthians 4:5–6*

If I say, "Surely the darkness will cover me, and the light around me turn to night," darkness is not dark to you, O God; the night is as bright as the day; darkness and light to you are both alike.   *Psalm 139:10–11*

The Officiant then says the Prayer for Light, using any one of the following or some other suitable prayer, first saying

Let us pray.

Almighty God, we give you thanks for surrounding us, as daylight fades, with the brightness of the vesper light; and we implore you of your great mercy that, as you enfold us with the radiance of this light, so you would shine into our hearts the brightness of your Holy Spirit; through Jesus Christ our Lord. *Amen.*

Grant us, Lord, the lamp of charity which never fails, that it may burn in us and shed its light on those around us, and that by its brightness we may have a vision of that holy City, where dwells the true and never-failing Light, Jesus the Christ. *Amen.*

O Lord God Almighty, as you have taught us to call the evening, the morning, and the noonday one day; and have made the sun to know its going down: Dispel the darkness of our hearts, that by your brightness we may know you to be the true God and eternal light, living and reigning for ever and ever. *Amen.*

Be our light in the darkness, O God, and in your great mercy defend us from all perils and dangers of this night; for the love of your only Son, our Savior Jesus Christ. *Amen.*

Advent

Collect for the First Sunday of Advent

Christmas, Epiphany, and other Feasts of the Incarnation

Collect for the First Sunday after Christmas

Lent and other times of penitence

Most merciful God, kindle within us the fire of love, that by its cleansing flame we may be purged of all our sins and made worthy to worship you in spirit and in truth; through Jesus Christ our Light. *Amen.*

Easter Season

Eternal God, who led your ancient people into freedom by a pillar of cloud by day and a pillar of fire by night: Grant that we who walk in the light of your presence may rejoice in the liberty of the children of God; through Jesus Christ our Savior. *Amen.*

Festivals of Saints

Lord Christ, your saints have been the lights of the world in every generation: Grant that we who follow in their footsteps may be made worthy to enter with them into that heavenly country where you live and reign for ever and ever. *Amen.*

The candles at the Altar are now lighted, as are other candles and lamps as may be convenient.

During the candle-lighting, an appropriate anthem or psalm may be sung, or silence kept.

The following hymn, or a metrical version of it, or Psalm 134, or Psalm 141, or some other hymn, is then sung

O Gracious Light   *Phos hilaron*

O gracious Light,
pure brightness of the everliving Father in heaven,
O Jesus Christ, holy and blessed!

Now as we come to the setting of the sun,
and our eyes behold the vesper light,
we sing your praises, O God: Father, Son, and Holy Spirit.

You are worthy at all times to be praised by happy voices,
O Son of God, O Giver of life,
and to be glorified through all the worlds.

or this

Psalm 134   *Ecce nunc*

Behold now, bless the LORD, all you servants of the LORD, *
   you that stand by night in the house of the LORD.
Lift up your hands in the holy place and bless the LORD; *
   the LORD who made heaven and earth bless
            you out of Zion.

or this

Psalm 141:1–3, 8ab   *Domine, clamavi*

O LORD, I call to you; come to me quickly; *
   hear my voice when I cry to you.
Let my prayer be set forth in your sight as incense, *
   the lifting up of my hands as the evening sacrifice.

Set a watch before my mouth, O LORD,
and guard the door of my lips; *
  let not my heart incline to any evil thing.
My eyes are turned to you, Lord GOD; *
  in you I take refuge.

The service may then continue in any of the following ways:

With Evening Prayer, beginning with the Psalms; or with some other Office or Devotion;

With the celebration of the Holy Eucharist, beginning with the Salutation and Collect of the Day;

Or, it may be followed by a meal or other activity, in which case Phos hilaron, or its alternative, may be followed by the Lord's Prayer and a grace or blessing;

Or, it may continue as a complete evening Office with the following elements:

Selection from the Psalter. Silence, or a suitable Collect, or both, may follow the Psalmody.

Bible Reading. A sermon or homily, a passage from Christian literature, or a brief silence, may follow the Reading.

Canticle. The Magnificat or other canticle, or some other hymn of praise.

Prayers. A litany, or other suitable devotions, including the Lord's Prayer.

Blessing or Dismissal, or both. The Peace may then be exchanged.

On feasts or other days of special significance, the Collect of the Day, or one proper to the season, may precede the Blessing or Dismissal. On other days, either of the following, or one of the Collects from Evening Prayer or from Compline, may be so used.

Blessed are you, O Lord our God, creator of the changes of day and night, giving rest to the weary, renewing the strength of those who are spent, bestowing upon us occasions of song in the evening. As you have protected us in the day that is past, so be with us in the coming night; keep us from every sin, every evil, and every fear; for you are our light and salvation, and the strength of our life. To you be glory for endless ages. *Amen.*

Almighty, everlasting God, let our prayer be set forth in your sight as incense, the lifting up of our hands as the evening sacrifice. Give us grace to behold you, present in your Word and Sacraments, and to recognize you in the lives of those around us. Stir up in us the flame of that love which burned in the heart of your Son as he bore his passion, and let it burn in us to eternal life and to the ages of ages. *Amen.*

A bishop or priest may use one of the following or some other blessing or grace

The Lord bless you and keep you. *Amen.*
The Lord make his face to shine upon you
   and be gracious to you. *Amen.*
The Lord lift up his countenance upon you
   and give you peace. *Amen.*

or this

May the blessing of the God of Abraham and Sarah, and of Jesus Christ born of our sister Mary, and of the Holy Spirit, who broods over the world as a mother over her children, be upon you and remain with you always. *Amen.*

A deacon or lay person using one of the preceding blessings substitutes "us" for "you."

A Dismissal may be used (adding "Alleluia, alleluia" in Easter Season)

The People respond

Thanks be to God.

In Easter Season the People respond

Thanks be to God. Alleluia, alleluia.

Daily Evening Prayer:
Rite Two *Adapted*

*The Officiant begins the service with one or more of the following
sentences of Scripture, or of those on pages 7–11;*

*or with the Service of Light on pages 36–40, and continuing with the
appointed Psalmody;*

or with one of the versicles on page 45

* Let my prayer be set forth in your sight as incense, the lifting
up of my hands as the evening sacrifice.   *Psalm 141:2*

Grace to you and peace from God our Father and from the
Lord Jesus Christ.   *Philippians 1:2*

Worship the LORD in the beauty of holiness; let the whole
earth tremble before him.   *Psalm 96:9*

* Yours is the day, O God, yours also the night; you established
the moon and the sun. You fixed all the boundaries of the
earth; you made both summer and winter.   *Psalm 74:15, 16*

I will bless the LORD who gives me counsel; my heart teaches
me, night after night. I have set the LORD always before me;
because God is at my right hand, I shall not fall.   *Psalm 16:7, 8*

Seek the One who made the Pleiades and Orion, and turns
deep darkness into the morning, and darkens the day into
night; who calls for the waters of the sea and pours them out
upon the surface of the earth: The LORD is God's name.   *Amos 5:8*

* If I say, "Surely the darkness will cover me, and the light around me turn to night," darkness is not dark to you, O God; the night is as bright as the day; darkness and light to you are both alike.   *Psalm 139:10, 11*

* Jesus said, "I am the light of the world; whoever follows me will not walk in darkness, but will have the light of life." *John 8:12*

The following Confession of Sin may then be said; or the Office may continue at once with one of the versicles on page 45.

Confession of Sin

The Officiant says to the people

Dear friends in Christ, here in the presence of Almighty God, let us kneel in silence, and with penitent and obedient hearts confess our sins, so that we may obtain forgiveness by God's infinite goodness and mercy.

or this

Let us confess our sins against God and our neighbor.

Silence may be kept.

Officiant and People together, all kneeling

Most merciful God,
we confess that we have sinned against you
in thought, word, and deed,
by what we have done,
and by what we have left undone.
We have not loved you with our whole heart;
we have not loved our neighbors as ourselves.
We are truly sorry and we humbly repent.
For the sake of our Savior Jesus Christ,
have mercy on us and forgive us;

that we may delight in your will,
and walk in your ways,
to the glory of your Name. Amen.

The priest alone stands and says

Almighty God have mercy on you, forgive you all your sins
through the grace of Jesus Christ, strengthen you in all
goodness, and by the power of the Holy Spirit keep you in
eternal life. *Amen.*

*A deacon or lay person using the preceding form remains kneeling, and
substitutes "us" for "you" and "our" for "your."*

The Invitatory and Psalter

All stand

Officiant	O God, be not far from us.
People	Come quickly to help us, O God.

or this

Officiant	O God, make speed to save us.
People	O Lord, make haste to help us.

Officiant and People

Glory to the Father, and to the Son, and to the Holy
Spirit; as it was in the beginning, is now, and will be for
ever. Amen.

Except in Lent, add   Alleluia.

or this

Honor and glory to the holy and undivided Trinity, God
who creates, redeems, and inspires; One in Three and Three
in One for ever and ever. Amen.

Except in Lent, add   Alleluia.

One of the following, or some other suitable hymn, or an Invitatory Psalm, may be sung or said

O Gracious Light *Phos hilaron*

O gracious Light,
pure brightness of the everliving Father in heaven,
O Jesus Christ, holy and blessed!

Now as we come to the setting of the sun,
and our eyes behold the vesper light,
we sing your praises, O God: Father, Son, and Holy Spirit.

You are worthy at all times to be praised by happy voices,
O Son of God, O Giver of life,
and to be glorified through all the worlds.

or this

Psalm 134 *Ecce nunc*

Behold now, bless the LORD, all you servants of the LORD, *
   you that stand by night in the house of the LORD.
Lift up your hands in the holy place and bless the LORD; *
   the LORD who made heaven and earth bless
            you out of Zion.

or this

Psalm 141:1–3, 8ab *Domine, clamavi*

O LORD, I call to you; come to me quickly; *
   hear my voice when I cry to you.
Let my prayer be set forth in your sight as incense, *
   the lifting up of my hands as the evening sacrifice.
Set a watch before my mouth, O LORD,
and guard the door of my lips; *
   let not my heart incline to any evil thing.
My eyes are turned to you, Lord GOD; *
   in you I take refuge.

Then follows

The Psalm or Psalms Appointed

At the end of the Psalms is sung or said

Glory to the Father, and to the Son, and to the Holy Spirit; as it was in the beginning, is now, and will be for ever. Amen.

or this

Honor and glory to the holy and undivided Trinity, God who creates, redeems, and inspires; One in Three and Three in One, for ever and ever. Amen

The Lessons

One or two Lessons, as appointed, are read, the Reader first saying

A Reading (Lesson) from _____.

A citation giving chapter and verse may be added.

After each Lesson the Reader may say

      The Word of the Lord.
Answer   Thanks be to God.

Or the Reader may say   Here ends the Lesson (Reading).

Silence may be kept after each Reading. One of the following Canticles, or one of those on pages 17–28, is sung or said after each Reading. If three Lessons are used, the Lesson from the Gospel is read after the second Canticle.

The Song of Mary   *Magnificat*

Luke 1:46–55

My soul proclaims the greatness of the Lord,
my spirit rejoices in God my Savior, *
    for you, Lord, have looked with favor on your lowly servant.
From this day all generations will call me blessed: *
    you, the Almighty, have done great things for me,
    and holy is your name.
You have mercy on those who fear you *
    from generation to generation.
You have shown strength with your arm *
    and scattered the proud in their conceit,
Casting down the mighty from their thrones *
    and lifting up the lowly.
You have filled the hungry with good things *
    and sent the rich away empty.
You have come to the aid of your servant Israel, *
    to remember the promise of mercy,
The promise made to our forebears, *
    to Abraham and his children for ever.

The Song of Simeon   *Nunc dimittis*

Luke 2:29–32

Lord, you now have set your servant free *
    to go in peace as you have promised;
For these eyes of mine have seen the Savior, *
    whom you have prepared for all the world to see:
A Light to enlighten the nations, *
    and the glory of your people Israel.

The Apostles' Creed

Officiant and People together, all standing

I believe in God, the Father almighty,
    creator of heaven and earth.
I believe in Jesus Christ, God's only Son, our Lord,
    who was conceived by the Holy Spirit,
    born of the Virgin Mary,
    suffered under Pontius Pilate,
    was crucified, died, and was buried;
    he descended to the dead.
    On the third day he rose again;
    he ascended into heaven,
    he is seated at the right hand of the Father,
    and he will come again to judge the living and the dead.
I believe in the Holy Spirit,
    the holy catholic Church,
    the communion of saints,
    the forgiveness of sins,
    the resurrection of the body,
    and the life everlasting. Amen.

The Prayers

The people stand or kneel

Officiant	Hear our cry, O God.
People	And listen to our prayer.
Officiant	Let us pray.

or this

Officiant	The Lord be with you.
People	And also with you.
Officiant	Let us pray.

Officiant and People

Our Father in heaven,
   hallowed be your Name,
   your kingdom come,
   your will be done,
     on earth as in heaven.
Give us today our daily bread.
Forgive us our sins
   as we forgive those who sin against us.
Save us from the time of trial,
   and deliver us from evil.
For the kingdom, the power, and the glory are yours,
   now and for ever. Amen.

Then follows one of these sets of Suffrages

A

V. Show us your mercy, O Lord;
R. And grant us your salvation.
V. Clothe your ministers with righteousness;
R. Let your people sing with joy.

V.   Give peace, O Lord, in all the world;
R.   For only in you can we live in safety.
V.   Lord, keep this nation under your care;
R.   And guide us in the way of justice and truth.
V.   Let your way be known upon earth;
R.   Your saving health among all nations.
V.   Let not the needy, O Lord, be forgotten;
R.   Nor the hope of the poor be taken away.
V.   Create in us clean hearts, O God;
R.   And sustain us with your Holy Spirit.

B

That this evening may be holy, good, and peaceful,
We entreat you, O God.

That your holy angels may lead us in paths of peace and
goodwill,
We entreat you, O God.

That we may be pardoned and forgiven for our sins and
offenses,
We entreat you, O God.

That there may be peace to your Church and to the whole
world,
We entreat you, O God.

That we may depart this life in your faith and fear, and not
be condemned before the great judgment seat of Christ,
We entreat you, O God.

That we may be bound together by your Holy Spirit in the
communion of [_____ and] all your saints, entrusting
one another and all our life to Christ,
We entreat you, O God.

The Collect of the Day

A Collect for Sundays

O God, whose Son our Savior Jesus Christ triumphed over the powers of death and prepared for us our place in the new Jerusalem: Grant that we, who have this day given thanks for his resurrection, may praise you in that City of which he is the light, and where he lives and reigns for ever and ever. *Amen.*

A Collect for Fridays

Lord Jesus Christ, by your death you took away the sting of death: Grant to us your servants so to follow in faith where you have led the way, that we may at length fall asleep peacefully in you and wake up in your likeness; for your tender mercies' sake. *Amen.*

A Collect for Saturdays

O God, the source of eternal light: Shed forth your unending day upon us who watch for you, that our lips may praise you, our lives may bless you, and our worship on the morrow give you glory; through Jesus Christ our Savior. *Amen.*

A Collect for Peace

Most holy God, the source of all good desires, all right judgments, and all just works: Give to us, your servants, that peace which the world cannot give, so that our minds may be fixed on the doing of your will, and that we, being delivered from the fear of all enemies, may live in peace and quietness; through the mercies of Christ Jesus our Savior. *Amen.*

A Collect for Aid against Perils

Be our light in the darkness, O God, and in your great mercy
defend us from all perils and dangers of this night; for the
love of your only Son, our Savior Jesus Christ. *Amen.*

A Collect for Protection

O God, the life of all who live, the light of the faithful, the
strength of those who labor, and the repose of the dead: We
thank you for the blessings of the day that is past, and
humbly ask for your protection through the coming night.
Bring us in safety to the morning hours; through him who
died and rose again for us, your Son our Savior Jesus Christ.
Amen.

A Collect for the Presence of Christ

Lord Jesus, stay with us, for evening is at hand and the day is
past; be our companion in the way, kindle our hearts, and
awaken hope, that we may know you as you are revealed in
Scripture and the breaking of bread. Grant this for the sake
of your love. *Amen.*

*Then, unless the Eucharist or a form of general intercession is to follow,
one of these prayers for mission is added*

O God and Maker of all, whom the whole heavens adore:
Let the whole earth also worship you, all nations obey you,
all tongues confess and bless you, and people everywhere
love you and serve you in peace; through Jesus the Christ.
Amen.

or the following

Keep watch, dear Lord, with those who work, or watch, or
weep this night, and give your angels charge over those who
sleep. Tend the sick, Lord Christ; give rest to the weary, bless
the dying, soothe the suffering, pity the afflicted, shield the
joyous; and all for your love's sake. *Amen.*

or this

O God, you manifest in your servants the signs of your
presence: Send forth upon us the Spirit of love, that in
companionship with one another your abounding grace may
increase among us; through Jesus the Christ. *Amen.*

Here may be sung a hymn or anthem.

Authorized intercessions and thanksgivings may follow.

Before the close of the Office one or both of the following may be used.

The General Thanksgiving

Officiant and People

Almighty God, Father of all mercies,
we your unworthy servants give you humble thanks
for all your goodness and loving-kindness
to us and to all whom you have made.
We bless you for our creation, preservation,
and all the blessings of this life;
but above all for your immeasurable love
in the redemption of the world by our Lord Jesus Christ;
for the means of grace, and for the hope of glory.
And, we pray, give us such an awareness of your mercies,
that with truly thankful hearts we may show forth your praise,
not only with our lips, but in our lives,
by giving up our selves to your service,
and by walking before you
in holiness and righteousness all our days;

through Jesus Christ our Lord,
to whom, with you and the Holy Spirit,
be honor and glory throughout all ages. Amen.

A Prayer of St. Chrysostom

Jesus our Savior, you have given us grace at this time with
one accord to make our common supplication to you; and
you have promised that when two or three are agreed in your
Name you will grant their requests: Fulfill now, O Lord, our
desires and petitions as may be best for us; granting us in this
world knowledge of your truth, and in the age to come life
everlasting. *Amen.*

Then may be said

Let us bless the Lord.
Thanks be to God.

*From Easter Day through the Day of Pentecost "Alleluia, alleluia" may be
added to the preceding versicle and response.*

The Officiant may then conclude with one of the following

The grace of our Lord Jesus Christ, and the love of God and
the fellowship of the Holy Spirit, be with us all evermore.
Amen.   *2 Corinthians 13:14*

May the God of hope fill us with all joy and peace in
believing through the power of the Holy Spirit. *Amen.*
Romans 15:13

Glory to God whose power, working in us, can do infinitely
more than we can ask or imagine: Glory to God from
generation to generation in the Church, and in Christ Jesus
for ever and ever. *Amen.*   *Ephesians 3:20, 21*

Additional Directions

Morning and Evening Prayer

Any of the opening sentences of Scripture, including those listed for specific seasons or days, may be used at any time, according to the discretion of the officiant.

The proper antiphons on pages 13–15 may be used as refrains with either of the two Invitatory Psalms, the Venite or the Jubilate.

Antiphons drawn from the Psalms themselves, or from the opening sentences given in the Offices, or from other passages of Scripture may be used with the morning Psalm 63, with the evening Psalms 134 and 141, and with the other Psalms and biblical Canticles.

The Gloria Patri or the "Honor and glory" is always sung or said at the conclusion of the entire portion of the Psalter; and may be used after the Invitatory Psalm, after the morning or evening psalm, or the Canticle "Christ our Passover," after each psalm, and after each section of Psalm 119.

After Canticles 8, 9, 9A, 10, 11, 12, 12A, 15, 15A, 16, 16A, 17, 19, 22, and 23, the Gloria Patri or the following theological equivalent may be sung or said:

Honor and glory to the holy and undivided Trinity, *
God who creates, redeems, and inspires:
One in Three and Three in One, *
for ever and ever. Amen.

The Additional Directions continue with "The following pointing of the Gloria. ." on page 141 and all that follows on pages 142 and 143 of the Book of Common Prayer.

The directions "Concerning the Service" and "Concerning the Celebration" on pages 74 and 108 of the Prayer Book apply also to these services.

The Holy Eucharist

Concerning this Eucharistic Rite

This eucharistic rite is newly composed following the classical pattern and the traditional content of the ancient Christian liturgical rites. It follows the familiar order of Rite Two in the Book of Common Prayer and is to be considered a supplement to it.

The intent of this rite is to enrich our liturgical prayer by making available a fuller array of images of God. As the People of God we are called to name God in our rites as we share in the worship of the whole creation offering praise to its Source.

The rite contains two newly composed eucharistic prayers (designated *First Supplemental Eucharistic Prayer* and *Second Supplemental Eucharistic Prayer*) and two new Prayers of the People (*Prayers of the People—First Supplement* and *Prayers of the People—Second Supplement*). The First Supplemental Eucharistic Prayer has as its theme the creation of all people in the image of God as the source of Christian inclusiveness. The Second Supplemental Eucharistic Prayer has the central metaphor of God bringing to birth and nourishing the whole creation.

Collects which echo the themes of the eucharistic prayers are included as alternatives to the Collect of the Day from the Book of Common Prayer.

The rubrics found in Concerning the Celebration on page 354 of the Book of Common Prayer are also applicable to this rite.

Additional directions are on page 82.

Please see also Commentary on Prayer Book Studies 30, a companion volume, for background and reference material for this service.

The Holy Eucharist

The Word of God

A hymn, psalm, or anthem may be sung.

The people standing, the Celebrant says

       Blessed be the one, holy, and living God.
People   Glory to God for ever and ever.

In place of the above, from Easter Day through the Day of Pentecost

Celebrant Alleluia. Blessed be our God.
People   Christ is risen. Alleluia.

In Lent and on other penitential occasions

Celebrant Blessed be the God of our salvation:
People   Who bears our burdens and forgives our sins.

When appointed, the following hymn or some other song of praise is sung or said, all standing

Splendor and honor and royal power
    are yours by right, O God Most High,
For you created everything that is,
    and by your will they were created and have their being;

And yours by right, O Lamb that was slain,
    for with your blood you have redeemed for God,
From every family, language, people, and nation,
    a royal priesthood to serve our God.

And so, to the One who sits upon the throne,
    and to Christ the Lamb,
Be worship and praise, dominion and splendor,
    for ever and for evermore.

On other occasions the following is used

Holy God,
Holy and Mighty,
Holy Immortal One,
Have mercy upon us.

The Collect of the Day

The Celebrant says to the people

              God be with you.   *or*   The Lord be with you.
People   And also with you.
Celebrant Let us pray.

The Celebrant says the Collect of the Day or one of the following Collects

Suggested for use with First Supplemental Eucharistic Prayer

O God, who wonderfully created and yet more wonderfully restored the dignity of human nature: Guide us in your grace that we may know and live the divine life of Christ, who reveals your majesty in our humanity; through your Anointed One, who lives and reigns with you and the Holy Spirit, one God, for ever and ever. *Amen.*

or this

O God, you have breathed new life into us through your Holy Spirit: Grant that we, reborn in your Name, anointed by your Spirit, and nourished in your Body, may burn with the fire of your love throughout the world; through the Risen Christ, who lives with you and the Holy Spirit, one God, for ever and ever. *Amen.*

Suggested for use with Second Supplemental Eucharistic Prayer

O God our creator, fountain of light and love and life: Be near to us and embrace us, and teach us to walk in your truth and your ways; through Jesus Christ who reigns in glory, with you and the Holy Spirit, now and for ever. *Amen.*

The Lessons

The people sit. One or two Lessons, as appointed, are read, the Reader first saying

A Reading (Lesson) from _____ .

A citation giving chapter and verse may be added.

After each Reading, the Reader may say

       The Word of the Lord.
People   Thanks be to God.

or the Reader may say   Here ends the Reading (Epistle).

Silence may follow.

A Psalm, hymn, or anthem may follow each Reading.

Then, all standing, the Deacon or a Priest reads the Gospel, first saying

       The Holy Gospel of our Savior Jesus Christ
       according to _____ .
People   Glory to you, Lord Christ.

After the Gospel, the Reader says

       The Gospel of the Lord.
People   Praise to you, Lord Christ.

The Sermon

The Nicene Creed

We believe in one God,
   the Father, the Almighty,
   maker of heaven and earth,
   of all that is, seen and unseen.

We believe in one Lord, Jesus Christ,
   the only Son of God,
   eternally begotten of the Father,
   God from God, Light from Light,
   true God from true God,
   begotten, not made,
   of one Being with the Father;
   through him all things were made.
   For us and for our salvation
     he came down from heaven,
     was incarnate of the Holy Spirit and the Virgin Mary
     and became truly human.
     For our sake he was crucified under Pontius Pilate;
     he suffered death and was buried.
     On the third day he rose again
     in accordance with the Scriptures;
     he ascended into heaven
     and is seated at the right hand of the Father.
     He will come again in glory to judge the living and the dead,
     and his kingdom will have no end.

We believe in the Holy Spirit, the Lord, the giver of life,
   who proceeds from the Father and the Son,
   who with the Father and the Son is worshiped and glorified,
   who has spoken through the prophets.
   We believe in one holy catholic and apostolic Church.
   We acknowledge one baptism for the forgiveness of sins.
   We look for the resurrection of the dead,
     and the life of the world to come. Amen.

The Prayers Of The People

Prayer is offered with intercession for

The Universal Church, its members, and its mission
The Nation and all in authority
The welfare of the world
The concerns of the local community
Those who suffer and those in any trouble
The departed (with commemoration of a saint when appropriate)

Prayer may be offered according to one of the forms on pages
77-79 of this book, or of those in the Book of Common Prayer
(pages 383-393).

Confession of Sin

A Confession of Sin is said here if it has not been said earlier. On
occasion, the Confession may be omitted.

The Deacon or Celebrant says

Let us confess our sins against God, our neighbor, and
ourselves.

Silence may be kept.

Minister and People

God of all mercy,
we confess that we have sinned against you,
resisting your will in our lives.
We have not honored you in ourselves, in each other,
and in the world which you have made.
Reach out your saving arm
and rescue us from our sin.

Forgive, restore, and strengthen us
through our Savior Jesus Christ,
that we may abide in your love
and serve only your will
for your people and all creation. Amen.

The Bishop when present, or the Priest, stands and says

Almighty God have mercy on you, forgive you all your sins
through the grace of Jesus Christ, strengthen you in all
goodness, and by the power of the Holy Spirit keep you in
eternal life. *Amen.*

The Peace

All stand. The Celebrant says to the people

        The peace of Christ be always with you.
People   And also with you.

*Then the Ministers and People may greet one another in the name of the
Risen Christ.*

The Holy Communion

The Celebrant may begin the Offertory with a sentence of Scripture.

During the Offertory, a hymn, psalm, or anthem may be sung.

*Representatives of the congregation bring the people's offerings of bread
and wine, and money or other gifts, to the deacon or celebrant. The
people stand while the offerings are presented and placed on the Altar.*

The Great Thanksgiving

A Second Supplemental form will be found on page 69.

First Supplemental Eucharistic Prayer

The people remain standing. The Celebrant, whether bishop or priest, faces them and sings or says

	The Lord be with you.
People	And also with you.
Celebrant	Lift up your hearts.
People	We lift them to the Lord.
Celebrant	Let us give thanks to the Lord our God.
People	It is right to give our thanks and praise.

Then, facing the Holy Table, the Celebrant proceeds

It is good and joyful that in your presence we give you thanks, Holy God, for you have included us in creation and made us in your glorious image. You have remembered us from our beginning and fed us with your constant love; you have redeemed us in Jesus Christ and knit us into one body. Through your Spirit you replenish us, and call us to fullness of life. Therefore, joining with angels and archangels and with all the faithful in every generation, we give voice to all creation as we sing (say):

Celebrant and People

Holy, holy, holy God of power and might,
heaven and earth are full of your glory.
 Hosanna in the highest.
Blessed is the one who comes in the name of our God.
 Hosanna in the highest.

Then the Celebrant continues

Most generous, self-giving God,
we celebrate your gift of creation.
We rejoice that you have formed us in your image
and called us to dwell in your infinite love.

You gave the world into our care
that we might be your faithful stewards
and reflect your bountiful grace.
Through Abraham and Sarah
you blessed us with a holy heritage.
You delivered us from slavery,
sustained us in the wilderness,
and raised up prophets
that we might realize the fullness of your promise.

But we failed to honor your image
in one another and in ourselves;
we failed to see your goodness in the world around us;
and so we violated your creation,
abused one another,
and rejected your love.
Yet you did not abandon us to sin and death,
but sent Jesus Christ to be our Savior.

United with us by incarnation
through Mary and the Holy Spirit,
and born into the human family,
he showed us the way of freedom and life.
Walking among us,
he touched us with healing and transforming power,
and showed us your glory.
Giving himself freely to death on the cross,
he triumphed over evil and became our salvation.

At the following words concerning the bread, the Celebrant is to hold it, or lay a hand upon it; and at the words concerning the cup, to hold or place a hand upon the cup and any other vessel containing wine to be consecrated.

On the night before he died for us,
our Savior Jesus Christ took bread,
and when he had given thanks to you,
he broke it, and gave it to his friends, saying:
"Take, eat:
This is my Body which is given for you.
Do this for the remembrance of me."

After supper, Jesus took the cup of wine,
and when he had given thanks,
he gave it to them, saying:
"Drink this, all of you:
This is my Blood of the new Covenant,
poured out for you and for all for the forgiveness of sins.
Whenever you drink it, do this for the remembrance of me."

In obedience to this command, O God:

Celebrant and People

We remember his death on the cross,
We proclaim the resurrection to new life,
We await the return of Christ in glory;

The Celebrant continues

And we present to you from your creation,
this bread and this wine.
By your Holy Spirit may they become for us
the bread of life and the cup of salvation,
the Body and Blood of our Savior Jesus Christ,
that we may be Christ's Body in the world.

Remember your holy people,
and, in the fullness of time,
welcome us into the everlasting heritage
of your sons and daughters,
that with [_____ and] all your saints,
past and yet to come,
we may praise your Name for ever.

Through Christ and with Christ and in Christ,
in the unity of the Holy Spirit
all honor and glory are yours, O God,
now and for ever. *AMEN.*

Continue with the Lord's Prayer on page 73.

Second Supplemental Eucharistic Prayer

The people remain standing. The Celebrant, whether bishop or priest, faces them and sings or says

	The Lord be with you.
People	And also with you.
Celebrant	Lift up your hearts.
People	We lift them to the Lord.
Celebrant	Let us give thanks to the Lord our God.
People	It is right to give our thanks and praise.

Then, facing the Holy Table, the Celebrant proceeds

We praise you and we bless you, O holy and living God,
Creator of heaven and earth.

One of the following proper prefaces is then sung or said

1. Of the First Person of the Trinity

For you create all things that are, that have been, and
that will be, made ever new and wondrous in your
love.

2. Of the Second Person of the Trinity

For you loved the world so much that you gave your Only-begotten, to take on human flesh and live among us: Jesus the Christ, our Savior.

3. Of the Third Person of the Trinity

For you breathed life into us and filled us with your Holy Spirit, our guardian and guide to fullness of life in Christ.

The celebrant then continues

Therefore we join in the chorus of praise that rings through eternity, with angels and archangels, prophets and martyrs, and all the holy men and women loved by you who have entered into joy. Together with them, we magnify you as we sing (say):

Holy, holy, holy God of power and might.
Heaven and earth are full of your glory.
   Hosanna in the highest.
Blessed is the one who comes in the name of our God.
   Hosanna in the highest.

Then the Celebrant continues

O God, from before time you made ready the creation. Through your Wisdom, your Spirit moved over the deep and brought to birth the heavens: sun, moon, and stars; earth, winds, and waters; growing things, both plants and animals; and finally humankind. You made us in your image, male and female, to love and care for the earth and its creatures as you love and care for us, your children.

You graced us with freedom of heart and mind, but we were heedless and willful. You took us by the hand, and taught us to walk in your ways. And though you led us with cords of compassion and bands of love, we wandered far away. Yet as a mother cares for her children, you would not forget us. Time and again you called us to live in the fullness of your love.

Then you acted anew in Creation. In order that we might see and know the riches of your grace, your Spirit entered into Mary, the maiden of Nazareth, that she might conceive and bear a Son, the holy child of God.

From Advent through the Day of Pentecost, the Celebrant continues according to the season

Advent: The world had waited long in pain and hope, and at last our Savior came to birth, fulfilling the promise of the reign of God in love.

Christmas: Jesus, from his humble and lowly birth, grew in wisdom and stature as the apple of your eye.

Epiphany: He came among us, that your holy light might shine in all the nations of the world.

Baptism: He came to the River Jordan, to be baptized by his cousin John, showing us the way to second birth into holiness and new life.

Lent: He came among us as one knowing weakness and temptation, yet did not sin.

Easter: He came among us, suffered and died, and rising to new life, opened the way into the New Creation.

Ascension: He ascended into heaven to fill all things, and to prepare a place for us.

Pentecost: When he had been raised from the dead, he filled us with the Spirit, your divine breath and fire, the wellspring of zeal, to live the gospel life.

The Celebrant continues

Living among us, Jesus loved us. He yearned to draw all the world to himself, as a hen gathers her young under her wings, yet we would not. We were heedless of his call to walk in love.

At the following words concerning the bread, the Celebrant is to hold it, or lay a hand upon it, and at the words concerning the cup, to hold or place a hand upon the cup and any other vessel containing wine to the consecrated.

At last the time came for him to make the sacrifice of himself, and to be glorified by you. On the night before he died, Jesus was at table with his friends. He took bread, gave thanks to you, broke it, and gave it to them, saying: "Take, eat: This is my Body, which is given for you. Do this for the remembrance of me."

After supper, Jesus took the cup of wine. Again he gave thanks to you, and gave it to them, saying: "Drink this, all of you: This is my Blood of the new Covenant, poured out for you and for all for the forgiveness of sins. Whenever you drink it, do this for the remembrance of me."

As we gather to share the bread and the cup, we remember this loving gift to us:

Celebrant and People

We remember his death on the cross,
We proclaim the resurrection to new life,
We await the return of Christ in glory;

And we join together in the love of Christ to give thanks and praise to you, our God. Here at this table we offer to you all that you have made: this bread and this cup, our (money and) time, and ourselves, a living sacrifice.

Pour out your love and your blessing on all we offer here. Breathe your Spirit into these gifts of bread and wine, to make of them the Body and Blood of Christ. Let your Spirit who broods over the whole creation dwell within us. Gather us to be your holy people, the Body of Christ given for the world you have made. Draw us, O God, to your heart at the heart of the world.

Through Christ and with Christ and in Christ, to whom, with you and the Holy Spirit, be honor and glory, now and for ever. *AMEN.*

As our Savior Christ has taught us, we now pray,

People and Celebrant

Our Father in heaven,
   hallowed be your Name,
   your kingdom come,
   your will be done,
      on earth as in heaven.
Give us today our daily bread.
Forgive us our sins
   as we forgive those who sin against us.
Save us from the time of trial,
   and deliver us from evil.
For the kingdom, the power, and the glory are yours,
   now and for ever. Amen.

The Breaking of the Bread

The Celebrant breaks the consecrated Bread.

A period of silence is kept.

Then may be sung or said

We are the body of Christ:
the broken body and the blood poured out.
We behold who we are;
may we become one with the One we receive.

or

We are one bread, one body.
We will love one another as Christ loves us.

In place of, or in addition to, the preceding, some other suitable anthem may be used.

Facing the people, the Celebrant says the following Invitation

The Gifts of God for the People of God.

and may add   Take them in remembrance that Christ died for you, and feed on him in your hearts by faith, with thanksgiving.

The ministers receive the Sacrament in both kinds, and then immediately deliver it to the people.

The Bread and the Cup are given to the communicants with these words

The Body of Christ, the bread of heaven. [*Amen.*]
The Blood of Christ, the cup of salvation. [*Amen.*]

During the ministration of Communion, hymns, psalms, or anthems may be sung.

When necessary, the Celebrant consecrates additional bread and wine, using the form on page 82.

After Communion, the Celebrant says

Let us pray.

For use with First Supplemental Eucharistic Prayer

Celebrant and People

Creator of all,
you have restored us in your image
through Jesus our Savior,
and you have united us in the Sacrament
of Christ's Body and Blood.
Sustain us in our lives of service
as a holy and consecrated body,
through Christ, our life and our joy. Amen.

or

For use with Second Supplemental Eucharistic Prayer

Celebrant and People

Holy, gracious, and loving God,
you have drawn us to your heart,
and nourished us at your table
with holy food and drink,
the Body and Blood of Christ.
Now send us forth
to be your people in the world,
and to proclaim your truth,
this day and evermore. Amen.

The Bishop when present, or the Priest, may bless the people.

The Deacon, or the Celebrant, dismisses them with these words

Let us go forth in the name of Christ.

People   Thanks be to God.

or this

Deacon   Let us go forth into the world, rejoicing in the
power of the Spirit.

People   Thanks be to God.

or this

Deacon   Let us bless the Lord.

People   Thanks be to God.

*From the Easter Vigil through the Day of Pentecost "Alleluia, alleluia"
may be added to either of the dismissals.*

The People respond   Thanks be to God. Alleluia, alleluia.

The Prayers of the People

Any of the forms which follow or those found on pages 383–393 of the Book of Common Prayer may be used.

A bar in the margin indicates petitions which may be omitted.

The particular prayers of the community may be inserted wherever a line in brackets appears.

Prayers of the People—First Supplement

Suggested for use with First Supplemental Eucharistic Prayer

Deacon or other leader

Beloved God, we thank you for giving us power through your Spirit to reveal your life to the world: strengthen, bless, and guide us to make you known by word and example. [_____ .]

We are your Church, O God.
Guide us in your grace.

We thank you for your creation, and pray for the earth you have given us to cherish and protect: nourish in us your love for all you have made. [_____ .]

We are your stewards, O God.
Guide us in your grace.

Guide and bless us in our work and in our play, and shape the patterns of our political and economic life, that all people may share in the fulfillment of your creative work. [_____ .]

We are your servants, O God.
Guide us in your grace.

> Awaken our hearts to your presence in all people; in
> those we love easily and those with whom we struggle, in
> those different from us and those familiar to us.
> [_____.]
>
> We are made in your image, O God.
> *Guide us in your grace.*
>
> We thank you for calling us to a glorious heritage as your
> holy people. Free us from lack of vision, from inertia of
> will and spirit. By your life-giving Spirit, lead us out of
> isolation and oppression, redeem and restore us.
> [_____.]
>
> You are the life within us, O God.
> *Guide us in your grace.*

We thank you for the gift of life, with all its blessings and
sorrows. Shield the joyous, comfort and strengthen those in
any need or trouble. [_____.] Bless those who will be
born today and those who will die, that joining with the
company of all your saints we may rejoice in one unending
song of praise.

In you alone we have eternal life, O God.
Guide us in your grace.

Celebrant

We offer these our prayers and thanksgivings to you,
O God, the source of all that is true and holy, now and
for ever. *Amen.*

Prayers of the People—Second Supplement

Suggested for use with Second Supplemental Eucharistic Prayer

Deacon or other leader

In trust, we bring before God our hopes and fears, our wonder and confusion, our joys and sorrows, asking God's blessing on our lives and the life of the world.

Let us pray. *(Silence)*

We pray for the Church, the family of Christ throughout the world, remembering particularly all the baptized who minister in this congregation and community. [Especially _____ .]

(Silence)

For the household of faith we pray:
Be with us and bless us, O God.

We pray for our nation. Endow us with your grace, and bring us to a more perfect union embracing young and old, rich and poor, men, women, and children, of all colors and cultures and tongues. [_____ .]

(Silence)

For our nation we pray:
Be with us and guide us, O God.

We pray for all nations, peoples, and tribes throughout the world. In your compassion lead us into the way of unity and peace, and bring us to that glorious liberty which is the birthright of all your children. [_____ .]

(Silence)

For the welfare of the world we pray:
Be with us and unite us, O God.

We pray for our neighbors in this community: at work, at school, and at play. Help us to be aware of those who are unemployed and without shelter, and give us compassion and determination to respond to their needs. [_____.]

(Silence)

For our community we pray:
Be with us and help us, O God.

We pray for everyone whose body aches, whose heart is weary or frightened, whose mind is confused or cast down. Strengthen with your healing Spirit all who suffer. [Especially _____.] Give us grace to be instruments of your peace.

(Silence)

For all who suffer and struggle we pray:
Be with us and heal us, O God.

We pray for all those who have died [especially _____]. Draw them to your bosom in love and to the new life of eternity, with [_____ and] all your saints, who have shown us how to live more fully the life of Christ.

(Silence)

For all who have entered new life in Christ's resurrection we pray:
Be with us and raise us, O God.

Celebrant

O God, who brought all things to birth in creation and gave us grace to become your daughters and sons: Draw us together that we may live in the Spirit as the family of Christ, to ages of ages. *Amen.*

Additional Directions

The Holy Table is spread with a clean white cloth during the celebration.

When the Great Litany is sung or said immediately before the Eucharist, the Litany concludes with the Kyries, and the Eucharist begins with the Salutation and the Collect of the Day. The Prayers of the People following the Creed may be omitted.

The hymn "Splendor and honor," or the hymn used in place of it, is sung or said from Christmas Day through the Feast of the Epiphany; on Sundays from Easter Day through the Day of Pentecost, on all the days of Easter Week, and on Ascension Day; and at other times as desired; but it is not used on the Sundays or ordinary weekdays of Advent or Lent.

The Trisagion, "Holy God," may be sung or said three times, or antiphonally.

The Sanctus found on page 362 of the Book of Common Prayer may be used in place of the Sanctus found in this rite.

The Additional Directions continue with those concerning the Lessons, and all that follows on pages 406–409 of the Prayer Book, except for the following:

Form for Consecrating Additional Elements

Hear us, most merciful God, and with your Word and Holy Spirit bless and sanctify this bread (wine) that it, also, may be the Sacrament of the precious Body (Blood) of Christ, who took bread (the cup) and said, "This is my Body (Blood)." *Amen.*

Musical Supplement

Prepared by the
Standing Commission on Church Music

Daily Morning Prayer:
Rite Two *Adapted*

Preces

Officiant:

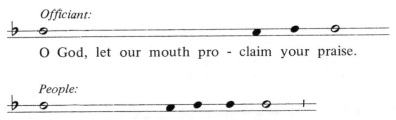

O God, let our mouth pro - claim your praise.

People:

And your glory all the day long.

Tones for the alternative Preces and the Gloria Patri can be found at S 51 in The Hymnal 1982.

Alternative doxological ending:

Officiant and People:

Honor and glory to the holy and undivided Trinity,

God who creates, redeems, and in - spires:

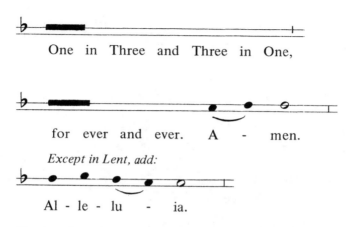

One in Three and Three in One,

for ever and ever. A - men.

Except in Lent, add:

Al - le - lu - ia.

The Antiphons for use with the Venite/Psalm 95 and the Jubilate may be set to music following the models in The Hymnal 1982 at S 294.

Settings for the Venite/Psalm 95 (S 34—S 40) from The Hymnal 1982 can be used with the substitution of "God's" for "his" in the last line. Settings of the Jubilate (S 41—S 45) and the Pascha nostrum (S 46—S 50) require no changes.

The alternative Morning Psalm may be sung to Plainsong or Anglican Chant according to the pointings below. If antiphons are desired for use with this psalm during Advent, Lent, or Easter, one of the appointed opening sentences for the season may be sung as an antiphon.

Psalm 63

Plainsong:

1   O *God,* you are my God; eagerly I séek you; *
   † my soul thirsts for you, my flesh faints for you,
      as in a barren and dry land where there is / no wáter.

2   Therefore I have gazed upon you in your hóly place, *
      that I might behold your power and / your glóry.

3 For your loving-kindness is better than lífe itself; *
   my lips / shall gíve you praise.

4 So will I bless you as long as I líve * ˏ
   and lift up my hands / in yóur Name.

5 My soul is content, as with marrow and fátness, *
   and my mouth praises you / with jóyful lips,

6 When I remember you upón my bed, *
   and meditate on you in the / night wátches.

7 For you have been my hélper, *
   and under the shadow of your wings / I ẃill
   rejoice.

8 My soul clíngs to you; *
   your right / hand hólds me fast.

Anglican Chant:

1 O God, you are my God;ˈ eagerly Iˈseek you; *
   my soul thirsts for you, my flesh faints for you,
   as in a barren and dryˈland where thereˈis
   noˈwater.

2 Therefore I have gazed upon you in yourˈholyˈplace, *
   that I might beˈhold yourˈpower and yourˈglory.

3 For your loving-kindness is better than ˈlife it ˈself; *
   my ˈlips shall ˈgive you ˈpraise.

4 So will I bless you as ˈlong as I ˈlive *
   and lift ˈup my ˈhands in your ˈName.

5 My soul is content, as with ˈmarrow and ˈfatness, *
   and my mouth ˈpraises you with ˈjoyful ˈlips,

6 When I remember you up ˈon my ˈbed, *
   and ˈmeditate on ˈyou in the ˈnight watches.

7 For you have ˈbeen my ˈhelper, *
   and under the shadow of your ˈwings I ˈwill
   re ˈjoice.

8 My ˈsöul ˈclings to you; *
   your ˈright hand ˈholds me ˈfast.

Morning Prayer Canticles

9A The First Song of Isaiah

Surely, it is ˈGod who ˈsaves me; *
   I will ˈtrust and will ˈnot be a ˈfraid.

The remaining verses as in The Hymnal 1982.

12A A Song of Creation

One or more sections of this Canticle may be used. Whatever the selection, it begins with the Invocation and concludes with the Doxology.

Invocation

1 Glorify the Lord, all you ⌐works of⌐ the ⌐Lord, *
    sing ⌐praise and⌐ give ⌐honor⌐ for ⌐ever.

2 In the high vault of heaven, ⌐glorify the⌐Lord, *
    sing ⌐praise and⌐ give ⌐honor⌐ for ⌐ever.

I The Cosmic Order

3 Glorify the Lord, you angels and all ⌐powers
                of the⌐Lord, *
    O heavens and all ⌐waters a⌐bove the⌐heavens.

4 Sun and moon and stars of the sky, ⌐glorify the⌐Lord, *
    sing ⌐praise and⌐ give ⌐honor⌐ for ⌐ever.

5 Glorify the Lord, every shower of ⌐rain and fall of⌐dew. *
    all ⌐winds and⌐fire and⌐heat.

6 Winter and summer, ⌐glorify the⌐Lord, *
    sing ⌐praise and⌐ give ⌐honor⌐ for ⌐ever.

7 Glorify the Lord, O ⌐chill and⌐cold, *
    drops of ⌐dew and⌐flakes of⌐snow.

8 Frost and cold, ice and sleet, ⌐glorify the⌐Lord, *
    sing ⌐praise and⌐ give ⌐honor⌐ for ⌐ever.

9 Glorify the Lord, O ⌐nights and⌐days, *
    O shining ⌐light and en⌐folding⌐dark.

10 Storm clouds and thunderbolts, 'glorify the 'Lord, *
    sing 'praise and give 'honor for 'ever.

II *The Earth and its Creatures*
11 Let the earth 'glorify the 'Lord, *
    sing 'praise and give 'honor for 'ever.
12 Glorify the Lord, O mountains and hills,
    and all that 'grows upon the 'earth, *
    sing 'praise and give 'honor for 'ever.

13 Glorify the Lord, O springs of water, 'seas, and 'streams, *
    O whales and 'all that 'move in the 'waters.
14 All birds of the air, 'glorify the 'Lord, *
    sing 'praise and give 'honor for 'ever.
15 Glorify the Lord, O 'beasts of the 'wild, *
    and 'all you 'flocks and 'herds.
16 O men and women everywhere, 'glorify the 'Lord, *
    sing 'praise and give 'honor for 'ever.

III *The People of God*
17 Let the people of God 'glorify the 'Lord, *
    sing 'praise and give 'honor for 'ever.
18 Glorify the Lord, O priests and 'servants
            of the 'Lord, *
    sing 'praise and give 'honor for 'ever.

19 Glorify the Lord, O spirits and 'souls of
        the 'righteous, *
    sing 'praise and give 'honor for 'ever.
20 You that are holy and humble of heart, 'glorify the 'Lord, *
    sing 'praise and give 'honor for 'ever.

Doxology
21 Let us glorify the Lord: Father, Son, and 'Holy 'Spirit: *
    sing 'praise and give 'honor for 'ever.
22 In the high vault of heaven, 'glorify the 'Lord, *
    sing 'praise and give 'honor for 'ever.

13A A Song of Praise

The settings (S 231-S 236) in The Hymnal 1982 *may be used by substituting "forebears" for "fathers" in the first line.*

14A A Song of Penitence

The small textual changes in verses 5 and 8 of this Canticle do not affect its Anglican Chant settings in The Hymnal 1982 *(S 238-S 241).*

15A The Song of Mary

1 My soul proclaims the greatness of the Lord,
    my spirit rejoices in 'God my 'Savior; *
        for you, Lord, have looked with 'favor
        on your 'lowly 'servant.

2 From this day all generations will ' call me ' blessèd: *
   you, the Almighty, have done great things for me,
   and ' holy ' is your ' Name.

3 You have mercy on ' those who ' fear you *
   from gener ' ation to ' gener ' ation.

4 You have shown ' strength with your ' arm *
   and scattered the ' proud in ' their con ' ceit,

5 casting down the ' mighty from their ' thrones *
   and ' lifting ' up the ' lowly.

6 You have filled the ' hungry with ' good things *
   and ' sent the ' rich away ' empty.

7 You have come to the aid of your ' servant ' Israel, *
   to re ' member the ' promise of ' mercy,

8 The promise ' made to our ' forebears, *
   to ' Abraham and his ' children for ' ever.

16A The Song of Zechariah

1 Blessèd are you, Lord, the ' God of ' Israel, *
   you have come to your ' people and ' set
   them ' free.

2 You have raised up for us a ' mighty ' Savior, *
   born of the ' house of your ' servant ' David.

3 Through your holy prophets you promised of old
   to ' save us from our ' enemies, *
   from the ' hands of ' all who ' hate us.

4 To show 'mercy to our 'forebears, *
    and to re 'member your 'holy 'covenant.

5 This was the oath you swore to our 'father 'Abraham: *
    to set us 'free from the 'hands of our 'enemies,

6 Free to worship you with 'out 'fear, *
    holy and righteous be 'fore you all the 'days of
    our 'life.

7 And you, child, shall be called the prophet of
    the 'Most 'High. *
    for you will go before the 'Lord to pre 'pare the 'way,

8 To give God's people 'knowledge of sal 'vation *
    by the for 'giveness 'of their 'sins.

9 In the tender com 'passion of our 'God *
    the dawn from on 'high shall 'break up 'on us,

10 To shine on those who dwell in darkness and
    the 'shadow of 'death, *
    and to guide our 'feet into the 'way of 'peace.

18A A Song to the Lamb

1 Splendor and honor and 'royal 'power *
    are yours by 'right, O 'God Most 'High,

2 For you created 'everything that 'is, *
    and by your will they were cre 'ated and 'have their 'being.

3 And yours by right, O 'Lamb that was 'slain, *
    for with your 'blood you have re 'deemed for 'God,

4 From every family, language,ˈpeople, andˈnation, *
   a royalˈpriesthood toˈserve ourˈGod.

5 And so, to the One whoˈsits upon theˈthrone, *
   —ˈand toˈChrist theˈLamb,

6 Be worship and praise, doˈminion andˈsplendor, *
   forˈever and forˈeverˈmore.

20A Glory to God

*By substituting "God's people" for "his people" in the first sentence,
the settings (S 272—S 281) in* The Hymnal 1982 *can be used for this
Canticle.*

21A You are God

1 We praise you, O God,
   we acˈclaim you asˈLord; *
     all creation worships you,
     theˈFatherˈeverˈlasting.

2 To you all angels, all theˈpowers ofˈheaven, *
     the cherubim and seraphim,ˈsing inˈendlessˈpraise:

3 Holy holy, holy Lord, God ofˈpower andˈmight, *
     heaven andˈearth areˈfull of yourˈglory.

4 The glorious company of aˈpostlesˈpraise you. *
     The nobleˈfellowship ofˈprophetsˈpraise you.

5 The white-robed army ofˈmartyrsˈpraise you. *
     Throughout the world theˈholyˈChurch acˈclaims you:

6   Father, of'majesty un'bounded, *
        your true and only Son,'worthy of'all'worship,
§7   the'Holy'Spirit, *
        —'advo'cate and'guide.

8   You, Christ, are the'king of'glory, *
        the e'ternal'Son of the'Father.
9   When you took our flesh to'set us'free *
        you humbly'chose the'Virgin's'womb.
10   You overcame the'sting of'death *
        and opened the kingdom of'heaven to'all be'lievers.
11   You are seated at God's'right hand in'glory. *
        We believe that you will'come to'be our'judge.
12   Come then, Lord, and'help your'people, *
        bought with the'price of'your own'blood,
13   and bring us'with your'saints *
        to'glory'ever'lasting.

§ *Second half of a double chant.*

22   A Song of Wisdom

1   Wisdom freed from a'nation of op'pressors *
        a holy'people and a'blameless'race.
2   She entered the soul of a'servant of the'Lord, *
        withstood dread'rulers with'wonders and'signs.

3 To the saints she gave the re'ward of their'labors, *
    and'led them by a'marvelous'way;
4 She was their'shelter by'day *
    and a'blaze of'stars by'night.

5 She brought them across the'Rëd'Sea, *
    she'led them through'mighty'waters;
6 But their enemies she'swallowed in the'waves *
    and spewed them'out from the'depths of the a'byss.

7 And then, Lord, the righteous sang'hymns to your'
    Name, *
    and praised with one'voice your pro'tecting'hand;
8 For Wisdom opened the'mouths of the'mute, *
    and gave speech to the'tongues of a'new-born'people.

23 A Song of Pilgrimage

1 Before I ventured forth,
    even while I was'very'young, *
    I sought wisdom'openly'in my'prayer.
2 In the forecourts of the temple I'asked for'her, *
    and I will'seek her'to the'end.
3 From first blossom to'early'fruit. *
    she has'been the de'light of my'heart.
4 My foot has kept firmly to the'true'path, *
    diligently from my'youth have'I pur'sued her.

§5 I inclined my ear a'little and re'ceived her; *
   I found for myself much'wisdom and be'came
   a'dept in her.

6 To the One who gives me wisdom'will I give'glory, *
   for I have resolved to'live ac'cording to her'way.

7 I have been'zealous for the'good, *
   in order that I'might not be'put to'shame.

8 My soul has'been subdued by'her, *
   and I have been'careful'in my'conduct.

9 I spread out my'hands to the'heavens, *
   and la'mented my'ignorance'of her.

10 I directed my'soul to'her, *
   and through purifi'cation'have I'found her.

11 From the beginning I gained'courage'from her, *
   therefore I'will not'be for'saken.

12 In my inmost being have I been'stirred to'seek her, *
   therefore have I'gained a'good pos'session.

13 As my reward the Almighty has given me the'gift
   of'language, *
   and with it will I'offer'praise to'God.

§ *Second half of a double chant.*

The Prayers

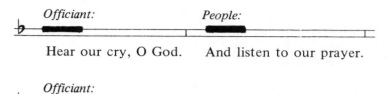

Hear our cry, O God. And listen to our prayer.

Let us pray.

The Tone for the Salutation and the Lord's Prayer can be found in The Hymnal 1982 *at S 51.*

Suffrages A will be found at S 52 in The Hymnal 1982

Suffrages B

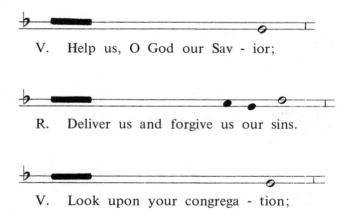

V.   Help us, O God our Sav - ior;

R.   Deliver us and forgive us our sins.

V.   Look upon your congrega - tion;

R. Give to your people the bless-ing of peace.

V. Declare your glory among the na - tions.

R. And your wonders among all peo - ples.

V. Let not the oppressed be shamed

and turned a - way.

R. Never forget the lives of your poor.

V. Continue your loving-kindness to

those who know you;

R. And your favor to those who are true of heart.

V. Satisfy us by your loving-kindness

in the morn - ing.

R. So shall we rejoice and be glad

all the days of our life.

Suffrages C

Cantor or Officiant:

V. Save your people, Lord, and

bless your inher - i - tance;

People:

R. Govern and uphold them, now and al - ways.

V. Day by day we bless you;

R. We praise your Name for ev - er.

V. Keep us today, Lord, from all sin.

R. Have mercy on us, Lord, have mer - cy.

V. Lord, show us your love and mer - cy;

R. For we have put our trust in you.

V. In you, Lord, is our hope.

R. Let us never be put to shame.

Settings for Collect Tone II (S 448) and for the Concluding Versicle and Response (S54—S55) will be found in The Hymnal 1982.

An Order of Worship for the Evening
Adapted

Settings for the first Greeting will be found at S 56 and S 57 in The Hymnal 1982.

From Easter Day through the Day of Pentecost:

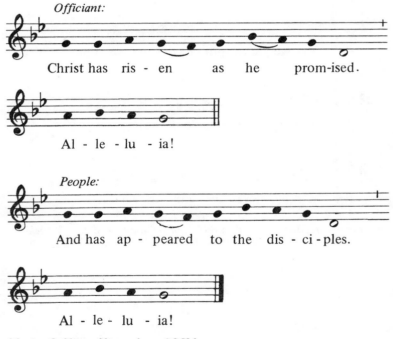

Officiant:

Christ has ris - en as he prom-ised.

Al - le - lu - ia!

People:

And has ap - peared to the dis - ci - ples.

Al - le - lu - ia!

Music: *O filii et filiae,* adapt. SCCM

Or this:

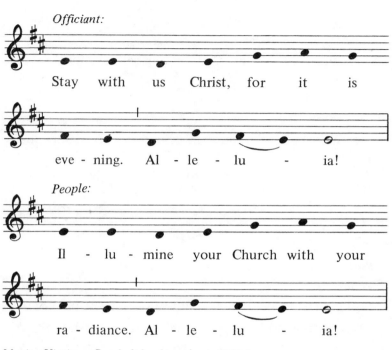

Music: *Victimae Paschali laudes,* adapt. SCCM

In Lent and other penitential occasions:

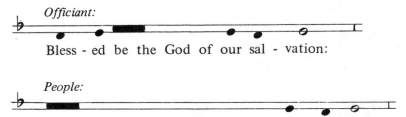

Officiant:

Bless - ed be the God of our sal - vation:

People:

Who bears our burdens and for - gives our sins.

A *Tone for the Short Lesson will be found at* S 449 *in* The Hymnal
1982. *The Collect Tones are at* S 447 *and* S 448.

Settings of the Phos hilaron can be found at S 59—S61 *in* The
Hymnal 1982.

Psalm 134

Plainsong:

Behŏld now, bless the LORD, all you sérvants óf the LORD, *
  you that stand by night in the/house of thë LORD.

Lift up your hands in the holy pláce and bléss the LORD; *
  the LORD who made heaven and earth bless you/out
  of Źion.

Anglican Chant:

Behold now, bless the LORD, all you ' sérvants of the ' LORD, *
  you that stand by ' night in the ' house of the ' LORD.

Lift up your hands in the holy place and ' bless the ' LORD; *
    the Lord who made heaven and earth ' bless you ' out
        of ' Zion.

Psalm 141:1-3, 8ab
Plainsong:
O LORD, I call to you; come to me quickly; *
    hear my voice/when I cry to you.

Let my prayer be set forth in your sight as incense, *
    the lifting up of my hands as the/evening sacrifice.

Set a watch before my mouth, O LORD,
and guard the door of my lips; *
    let not my heart incline to/any evil thing.

My eyes are turned to you, Lord GOD; *
    in/you I take refuge.

Anglican Chant:
O LORD, I call to you; ' come to me ' quickly; *
    hear my ' voïce ' when I ' cry to you.

Let my prayer be set forth in your ' sight as ' incense, *
    the lifting up of my ' hands as the ' evening ' sacrifice.

Set a watch before my mouth, O LORD,
and guard the ' door of my ' lips; *
    let not my heart incline to ' any ' evil ' thing.

My eyes are turned to ' you, Lord ' GOD; *
in ' you I ' take ' refuge.

Tones for the Aaronic Blessing will be found in the Musical Appendix of the Altar Book, which also contains the Tone for Blessings.

Tones for Dismissals (S 174—S 176) are in The Hymnal 1982.

Daily Evening Prayer:
Rite Two *Adapted*

Preces

Officiant:

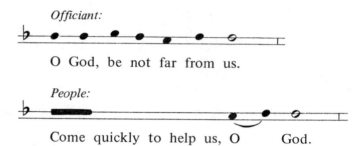

O God, be not far from us.

People:

Come quickly to help us, O   God.

The alternative Preces will be found at S 58 in The Hymnal 1982; *the alternative to the Gloria Patri will be found in the settings for Daily Morning Prayer: Rite Two* Adapted *(p. 84). For the Phos hilaron or alternative Psalms see The Order of Worship for Evening* Adapted *(p. 102).*

The pointing of the Magnificat for Anglican Chant can be found at Canticle 15A in Daily Morning Prayer: Rite Two Adapted *(p. 90). Settings for the Nunc dimittis (S 253—S 260, S 405) can be found in* The Hymnal 1982.

The Prayers

The Versicle and Response before the Lord's Prayer are the same as in Daily Morning Prayer: Rite Two Adapted *(p. 97). A Tone for the Salutation will be found in* The Hymnal 1982 *at S 62.*

For Suffrages A, see S 52 in The Hymnal 1982. Two Tones (S 63—S 64) are also provided there for Suffrages B, which can be used for the adapted rite by substituting "God" for "Lord" in the People's response.

The Tone for the Collects (S 448) and ones for the concluding Versicle and Response (S 65—S 66) can be found in The Hymnal 1982.

The Holy Eucharist

Opening Acclamation

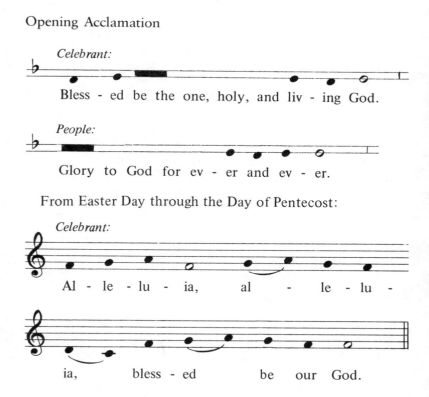

Celebrant:

Bless - ed be the one, holy, and liv - ing God.

People:

Glory to God for ev - er and ev - er.

From Easter Day through the Day of Pentecost:

Celebrant:

Al - le - lu - ia, al - le - lu -

ia, bless - ed be our God.

People:

Christ is ris - en, al - le - lu - ia, al - le - lu - ia.

Music: Alleluia VI

For the Lenten Acclamation, see Order of Worship for Evening, (p. 104)

For the Anglican Chant pointing of the Song of Praise, see Canticle 18A (p. 92). Settings of The Trisagion (S 99-S 102, S 360) will be found in The Hymnal 1982.

The Peace

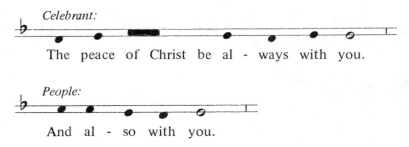

Celebrant:

The peace of Christ be al - ways with you.

People:

And al - so with you.

The Sursum corda in the Supplemental Eucharistic Prayers can be sung to S 120 in The Hymnal 1982 by substituting "our" for "him" in the last response of the People.

The Preface: First Supplemental Eucharistic Prayer

It is good and joy - ful that in your presence we give you thanks, Ho - ly God. for you have included us in cre - a - tion and made us in your glo - rious im - age. You have remembered us from our be - gin - ning and fed us with your

con - stant love; you have redeemed us in

Je - sus Christ and knit us in - to one

bod – y. Through your Spirit you re - plen - ish

us, and call us to full - ness

of life. There - fore, join-ing with angels

and arch - an - gels and with all the

faithful in every gen - er - a - tion,

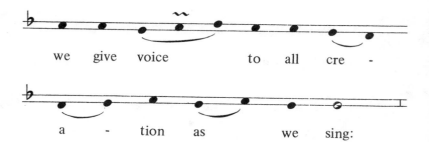

we give voice to all cre -

a - tion as we sing:

The Preface: Second Supplemental Eucharistic Prayer

One of the following proper prefaces is sung:

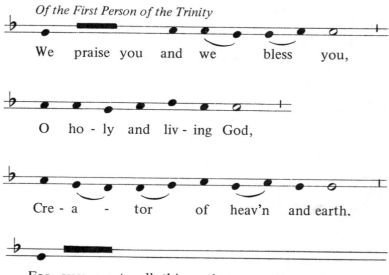

Of the First Person of the Trinity

We praise you and we bless you,

O ho - ly and liv - ing God,

Cre - a - tor of heav'n and earth.

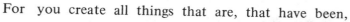

For you create all things that are, that have been,

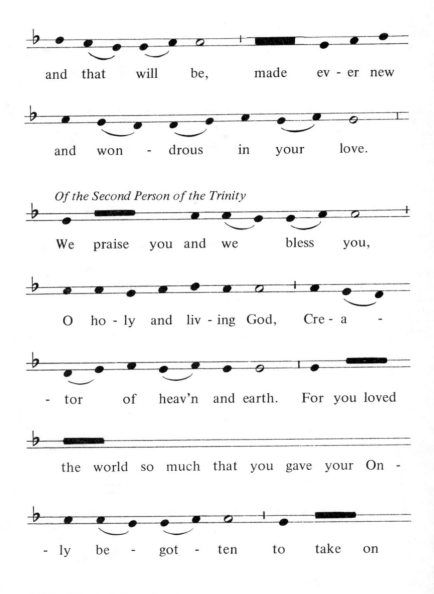

and that will be, made ev - er new

and won - drous in your love.

Of the Second Person of the Trinity

We praise you and we bless you,

O ho - ly and liv - ing God, Cre - a -

- tor of heav'n and earth. For you loved

the world so much that you gave your On -

- ly be - got - ten to take on

human   flesh   and   live   a   -   mong   us:

Je - sus   the   Christ,   our   Sav -   ior.

Of the Third Person of the Trinity

We   praise   you   and   we   bless   you,

O   ho - ly   and   liv - ing   God,   Cre - a -

- tor   of   heav'n   and   earth.   For   you

breathed   life   in -   to   us   and   filled

us   with   your   Ho - ly   Spir   -   it,

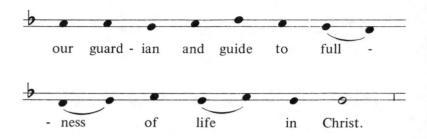

our guard - ian and guide to full -

- ness of life in Christ.

The Celebrant then continues:

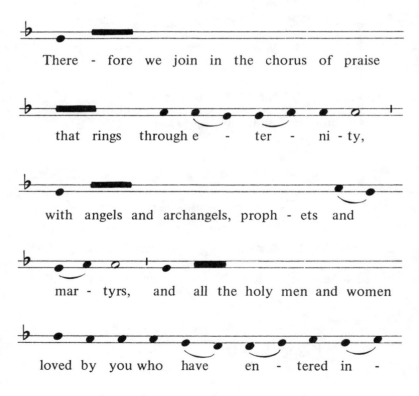

There - fore we join in the chorus of praise

that rings through e - ter - ni - ty,

with angels and archangels, proph - ets and

mar - tyrs, and all the holy men and women

loved by you who have en - tered in -

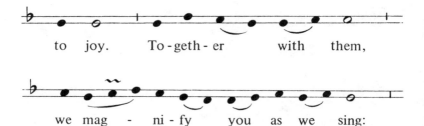

to joy. To-geth-er with them,

we mag - ni-fy you as we sing:

S 124 Adapted

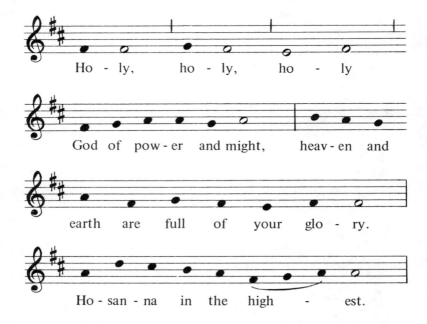

Ho - ly, ho - ly, ho - ly

God of pow-er and might, heav-en and

earth are full of your glo - ry.

Ho - san - na in the high - est.

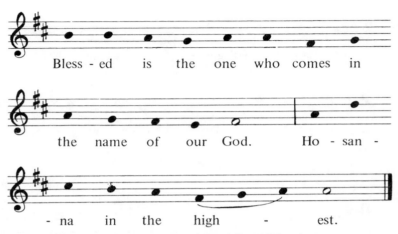

Bless - ed is the one who comes in

the name of our God. Ho - san -

- na in the high - est.

Setting: from *New Plainsong;* David Hurd (b. 1950), adapt.
Copyright © 1981, G.I.A. Publications, Inc.

S 125 Adapted

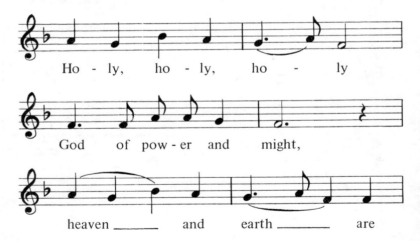

Ho - ly, ho - ly, ho - ly

God of pow - er and might,

heaven _____ and earth _____ are

full of your glory. Ho -

- san - na in the high - est. Ho -

- san - na in the high - est.

Bless - ed is the one who comes in the

name of our God. Ho -

- san - na in the high - est. Ho -

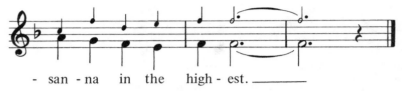

san - na in the high - est. _____

Setting: From *A Community Mass*; Richard Proulx (b. 1937), adapt.
Copyright © 1971, 1977, G.I.A. Publications, Inc.

S 128 Adapted

Ho - ly,

ho - ly, ho - ly

God of power _ and might, _____

heaven and earth are full of your glo - ry.

Ho-san - na in the high - est.

Bless - ed is the one who comes in the name of our God.

Ho - san - na in the high - est.

Setting: William Mathias (b. 1934), adapt.
Copyright © 1976, Oxford University Press, Inc.

S 130 Adapted

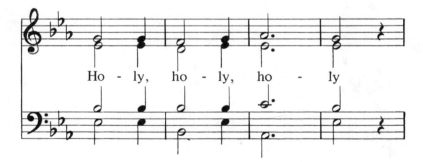

Ho - ly, ho - ly, ho - ly

God of power and might, _____

Ho - ly, ho - ly, ho - ly

God of power and might, _____

heav - en and earth are full,_____

full ____ of your glo -

- ry. Ho - san - na in the

high - est. Ho - san - na

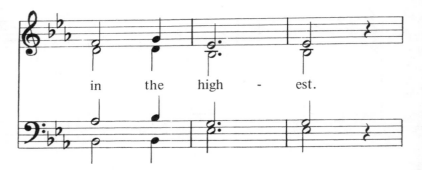

in the high - est.

bless - ed is the one who comes _____

in the name of our

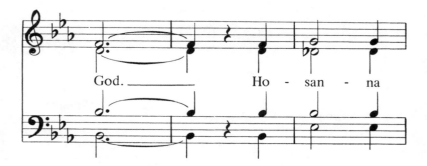

God. _____ Ho - san - na

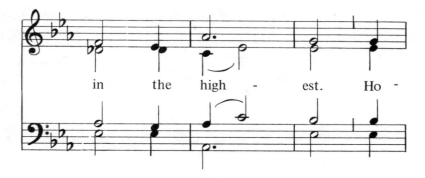

in the high - est. Ho -

- san - na in the high - est.

Setting from *Deutche Messe*, Franz Peter Schubert (1797-1828):
arr. Richard Proulx (b. 1937), adapt.
Adaptation copyright © 1985, G.I.A. Publications, Inc.

Conclusion of the Eucharistic Prayer

First Supplemental Prayer

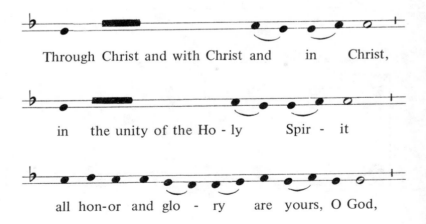

Through Christ and with Christ and in Christ,

in the unity of the Ho - ly Spir - it

all hon-or and glo - ry are yours, O God,

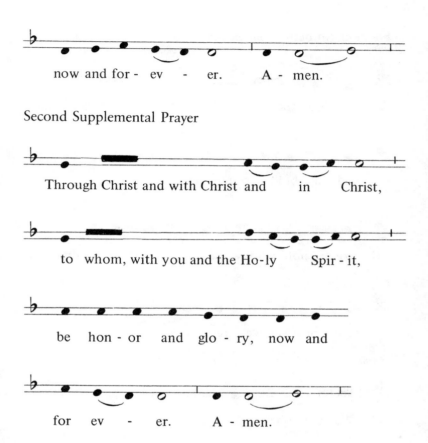

now and for - ev - er. A - men.

Second Supplemental Prayer

Through Christ and with Christ and in Christ,

to whom, with you and the Ho-ly Spir - it,

be hon - or and glo - ry, now and

for ev - er. A - men.

Fraction Anthem *This anthem may be sung in full by all, or by the choir, or as a versicle and response.*

V. We are the body of Christ: the broken body

and the blood poured out.

R. We be-hold who we are; may we become one

with the One we re - ceive.

or this

V. We are one bread, one bo - dy.

R. We will love one another as Christ loved us.

Tones for the Invitation to Communion and for Blessings can be found in the Musical Appendix of the Altar Book. Tones for Dismissals (S 174—S 176) are in The Hymnal 1982.

Prayers of the People: First Form

This form of the Prayers of the People can be sung according to the following formula:

Deacon or Cantor:

Beloved God, . . .   We are your Church, O God.
We thank you . . .   We are your servants, O God.
Etc.

People:

Guide us   in your grace.

The People's response may be sung in parts:

Guide us   in   your grace.

As may the Amen:

A - men.

The Celebrant's concluding prayer may be monotoned or sung to Collect Tone II (S 448).